100 *fast* fillets

chicken · fish · beef · lamb · pork

THE AUSTRALIAN
Women's Weekly

Contents

The fillet is a fine cut of meat. It needs no trimming plus it's adaptable, quick to cook and very, very forgiving (do as much or as little to it as you like and it still tastes great). Here, we've come up with a hundred top ideas that add taste-tempting versatility to the fillet as a main course, each appealingly different to the next. And if this weren't sensational enough, these recipes can be on the table in no time at all.

Pamela Clark

Food Director

Chicken fillets

Not just popular because it tastes so good, chicken is loaded with protein and essential vitamins. Our top tip is to avoid overcooking your chook as this will only make it dry; perfectly cooked poultry is always moist.

almond and coriander chicken with lemon mayonnaise

prep time 15 minutes   cook time 10 minutes   serves 4

1½ cups (180g) almond meal

2 teaspoons dried chilli flakes

½ cup finely chopped fresh coriander

1 tablespoon finely grated lemon rind

2 eggs

4 x 200g breast fillets

⅓ cup (50g) plain flour

vegetable oil, for shallow-frying

lemon mayonnaise

⅔ cup (200g) mayonnaise

1 teaspoon finely grated lemon rind

¼ cup (60ml) lemon juice

1 Preheat oven to 220°C/200°C fan-forced.

2 Make lemon mayonnaise.

3 Combine meal, chilli, coriander and rind in shallow medium bowl. Whisk eggs lightly in another shallow medium bowl. Coat chicken in flour, shake off excess. Dip chicken in egg then coat in meal mixture.

4 Heat oil in large frying pan; cook chicken, in batches, until browned. Place chicken on oven tray; bake, uncovered, about 10 minutes or until cooked. Slice chicken into thick pieces; serve with mayonnaise.

lemon mayonnaise Combine ingredients in small bowl.

per serving 81.8g total fat (11.1g saturated fat); 4402kJ (1053 cal); 21.6g carbohydrate; 57.2g protein; 5.2g fibre

chicken with roasted cherry tomato and basil sauce

prep time 5 minutes cook time 25 minutes serves 4

500g cherry tomatoes
5 cloves garlic, unpeeled
2 tablespoons olive oil
4 x 200g breast fillets
¼ cup coarsely chopped fresh basil
¼ cup (60ml) cream

1 Preheat oven to 200°C/180°C fan-forced.

2 Combine tomatoes, garlic and oil in large shallow baking dish. Roast, uncovered, about 20 minutes or until tomatoes soften. When garlic is cool enough to handle, peel.

3 Meanwhile, cook chicken on heated oiled grill plate (or grill or barbecue) until cooked through. Cover; stand 5 minutes.

4 Blend or process garlic and half the tomatoes until smooth. Place in medium saucepan with basil and cream; cook, stirring, over low heat, until heated through. Serve chicken topped with sauce and remaining tomatoes.

per serving 26.8g total fat (9g saturated fat); 1818kJ (435 cal); 3.6g carbohydrate; 44g protein; 2.7g fibre

creamy herb and garlic chicken with gnocchi

prep time 5 minutes cook time 20 minutes serves 4

Gnocchi, Italian "dumplings" made of potato, semolina or flour, are simple to prepare at home, but when you're pressed for time, they can be purchased in the fresh pasta section of most supermarkets.

1 tablespoon olive oil
4 x 200g breast fillets
500g fresh gnocchi
2 cloves garlic, crushed
300ml cream
1 tablespoon lemon juice
2 tablespoons finely chopped fresh oregano

1 Heat half the oil in large frying pan; cook chicken, uncovered, about 15 minutes or until cooked through.
2 Meanwhile, cook gnocchi in large saucepan of boiling water, uncovered, until just tender; drain.
3 Heat remaining oil in same frying pan; cook garlic, stirring, 1 minute. Add cream and juice; bring to a boil. Reduce heat; simmer, uncovered, about 5 minutes or until mixture thickens slightly. Remove from heat; stir in oregano.
4 Slice chicken into thick pieces. Divide gnocchi among serving plates, top with chicken, drizzle with sauce.

per serving 49.2g total fat (26g saturated fat); 3344kJ (800 cal); 38.8g carbohydrate; 49.6g protein; 3.1g fibre

piri piri chicken thigh fillets

prep time 10 minutes cook time 15 minutes serves 4

Piri piri, the spicy Afro-Portuguese chilli paste, seems made to enliven grilled poultry.

4 fresh long red chillies, chopped coarsely
1 teaspoon dried chilli flakes
2 cloves garlic, quartered
1 teaspoon sea salt
2 tablespoons olive oil
1 tablespoon apple cider vinegar
2 teaspoons brown sugar
8 x 125g thigh fillets

1 Using mortar and pestle, grind fresh chilli, chilli flakes, garlic and salt to make piri piri paste.
2 Combine paste with oil, vinegar, sugar and chicken in medium bowl. Cook chicken on heated oiled grill plate (or grill or barbecue) until cooked through. Serve with lime wedges, if desired.

per serving 27.2g total fat (6.8g saturated fat); 1822kJ (436 cal); 1.8g carbohydrate; 46.6g protein; 0.3g fibre

creamy horseradish chicken with garlic sautéed spinach

prep time 10 minutes cook time 20 minutes serves 4

Horseradish, a strong-flavoured member of the mustard family, is sold in various forms; be certain to use the unadulterated bottled version here rather than horseradish cream. You need 4 large bunches of spinach weighing about 1.6 kilos to get the amount of trimmed spinach required for this recipe.

1 tablespoon olive oil
4 x 200g breast fillets
1 green onion, sliced thinly
2 tablespoons dry white wine
⅔ cup (160ml) cream
2 tablespoons prepared horseradish
2 teaspoons lemon juice
½ teaspoon dijon mustard
1 teaspoon finely chopped fresh dill
20g butter
2 cloves garlic, crushed
600g trimmed spinach, chopped coarsely

1 Heat half the oil in large frying pan; cook chicken until cooked through. Remove from pan; cover to keep warm.

2 Heat remaining oil in same heated pan. Add onion; cook, stirring, until soft. Add wine; bring to a boil. Reduce heat; simmer, uncovered, until liquid is reduced by half. Add cream; bring to a boil. Reduce heat; simmer, uncovered, about 2 minutes or until sauce thickens slightly. Add horseradish, juice, mustard and dill; stir over heat until heated through.

3 Meanwhile, melt butter in large saucepan. Add garlic; cook, stirring, 2 minutes. Add spinach; cook over low heat, covered, about 2 minutes or until wilted.

4 Serve chicken and spinach drizzled with sauce.

per serving 38.6g total fat (18.8g saturated fat); 2366kJ (566 cal); 4g carbohydrate; 47.6g protein; 4.6g fibre

parmesan and couscous chicken strips

prep time 10 minutes   cook time 30 minutes   serves 4

Couscous originated in North Africa, where it is traditionally served as an accompaniment to local thick, hearty stews known as tagines.

1 cup (200g) couscous
¼ cup (20g) finely grated parmesan cheese
2 tablespoons finely chopped fresh
   flat-leaf parsley
1 teaspoon finely grated lemon rind
2 eggs
800g breast fillets, sliced thickly crossways
⅓ cup (50g) plain flour
⅔ cup (200g) mayonnaise
2 cloves garlic, crushed
vegetable oil, for shallow-frying

1 Combine couscous, cheese, parsley and rind in shallow medium bowl. Whisk eggs lightly in another shallow medium bowl. Coat chicken in flour, shake off excess. Dip chicken in egg then in couscous mixture.
2 Combine mayonnaise and garlic in small bowl.
3 Heat oil in large frying pan; cook chicken, in batches, until cooked through. Drain on absorbent paper. Serve chicken with garlic mayonnaise.
per serving 73.7g total fat (12.4g saturated fat); 5463kJ (1307 cal); 93.7g carbohydrate; 62.2g protein; 11.7g fibre

chicken, bocconcini and olive pizza

prep time 10 minutes   cook time 25 minutes   serves 4

We used large, 25cm diameter, packaged pizza bases for this recipe.

400g breast fillets
2 x 335g pizza bases
½ cup (130ml) bottled tomato pasta sauce
½ cup (75g) seeded black olives
250g cherry tomatoes, halved
210g cherry bocconcini, sliced thinly
2 tablespoons basil pesto
½ cup firmly packed fresh basil leaves

1 Preheat oven to 240°C/220°C fan-forced.
2 Cook chicken, uncovered, in heated oiled large frying pan until cooked through. Remove from pan; slice thinly.
3 Meanwhile, place pizza bases on oven trays; spread pasta sauce evenly over bases. Sprinkle chicken, olives, tomato and cheese over bases.
4 Bake about 15 minutes or until bases are crisp. Drizzle pesto over pizzas, sprinkle with basil.
per serving 24.2g total fat (8.7g saturated fat); 3407kJ (815 cal); 96.7g carbohydrate; 47.4g protein; 8.3g fibre

moroccan chicken with pistachio couscous

prep time 20 minutes   cook time 15 minutes   serves 4

1 teaspoon ground cumin
1 teaspoon ground coriander
½ teaspoon sweet smoked paprika
¼ teaspoon ground turmeric
¼ teaspoon cayenne pepper
2 teaspoons finely grated lemon rind
600g thigh fillets
1 medium red capsicum (200g), sliced thinly
1½ cups (300g) couscous
1⅓ cups (330ml) boiling water
⅓ cup (80ml) lemon juice
2 tablespoons olive oil
½ cup (70g) roasted pistachios, chopped coarsely
½ cup firmly packed fresh coriander leaves

1 Combine spices, rind and chicken in large bowl, rubbing spice mixture firmly into chicken. Cook chicken, uncovered, in heated oiled large frying pan until cooked through. Remove chicken from pan; slice thickly.
2 Add capsicum to same cleaned heated pan; cook, stirring, 1 minute.
3 Meanwhile, combine couscous and the water in large heatproof bowl. Cover, stand about 5 minutes or until liquid is absorbed, fluffing with fork occasionally; stir in juice and oil.
4 Stir nuts and coriander into couscous; toss gently to combine. Serve couscous topped with chicken and capsicum.
per serving 29.3g total fat (5.7g saturated fat); 2876kJ (688 cal); 62.4g carbohydrate; 41.9g protein; 3.2g fibre

salt and pepper crisp-skinned chicken

prep time **15 minutes** cook time **30 minutes** serves **4**

If you've ever brunched on yum cha, you've probably eaten gai lan – and loved it; stir-fried or steamed then splashed with a little sesame oil and oyster sauce. This deliciously crunchy vegetable is the perfect accompaniment to our crisp-skinned chicken.

2 teaspoons sea salt

2 teaspoons cracked black peppercorns

1 teaspoon dried chilli flakes

4 x 200g breast fillets, skin on

400g gai lan, chopped coarsely

1 tablespoon oyster sauce

2 teaspoons sesame oil

¼ cup firmly packed fresh coriander leaves

2 green onions, sliced thinly

1 Combine salt, pepper, chilli and chicken in large bowl.

2 Cook chicken, skin-side down, in heated oiled wok, about 10 minutes or until browned and crisp. Turn chicken; cook about 5 minutes or until cooked through. Remove from wok; cover to keep warm.

3 Stir-fry gai lan, sauce and oil in same heated wok until gai lan is wilted.

4 Serve chicken with gai lan, sprinkled with coriander and onion.

per serving 15.9g total fat (4.1g saturated fat); 1400kJ (335 cal); 2.8g carbohydrate; 44.3g protein; 1.8g fibre

steamed spinach-wrapped chicken with anchovy and tomato

prep time 15 minutes cook time 20 minutes serves 4

You need a large bunch of spinach weighing about 400g to get the number of large leaves required for this recipe.

24 large trimmed spinach leaves (150g)
4 anchovy fillets, drained, chopped finely
2 tablespoons rinsed baby capers, drained
1 tablespoon olive oil
¼ cup (35g) drained semi-dried tomatoes, chopped coarsely
½ teaspoon cracked black pepper
2 cloves garlic, crushed
4 x 200g breast fillets
lemon dressing
2 tablespoons olive oil
1 teaspoon finely grated lemon rind
2 tablespoons lemon juice
1 clove garlic, crushed

1 Bring large saucepan of water to a boil; add spinach, one leaf at a time, drain immediately. Place in large bowl of iced water, stand 3 minutes. Drain spinach thoroughly on absorbent paper.
2 Combine anchovy, capers, oil, tomato, pepper and garlic in small bowl.
3 Divide spinach into four portions; spread leaves flat on board. Place one chicken fillet on each spinach portion. Top chicken with anchovy mixture. Wrap spinach around chicken to completely enclose.
4 Place chicken parcels in baking-paper-lined bamboo steamer set over large saucepan of simmering water; steam, covered, about 20 minutes or until chicken is cooked through.
5 Meanwhile, whisk ingredients for lemon dressing in small bowl. Serve chicken with dressing.
per serving 26.1g total fat (5.6g saturated fat); 1894kJ (453 cal); 4.4g carbohydrate; 49.2g protein; 2.5g fibre

thai chicken noodle broth

prep time 15 minutes cook time 15 minutes serves 4

1 litre (4 cups) chicken stock
2 cups (500ml) water
3cm piece fresh ginger (15g), grated
1 fresh small red thai chilli, chopped finely
400g breast fillets, sliced thinly
400g fresh rice noodles
1 tablespoon fish sauce
1 tablespoon grated palm sugar
1 tablespoon lime juice
2 baby buk choy (300g), quartered
⅓ cup loosely packed fresh thai basil leaves

1 Combine stock, the water, ginger and chilli in large saucepan; cover, bring to a boil. Reduce heat; simmer 5 minutes. Add chicken, noodles, sauce, sugar and juice; simmer, about 5 minutes or until chicken is cooked through and noodles are tender.
2 Divide buk choy among serving bowls; ladle chicken broth into bowls. Sprinkle with basil.
per serving 7.1g total fat (2.2g saturated fat); 1208kJ (289 cal); 27.5g carbohydrate; 27.6g protein; 1.7g fibre

chicken with pecan honey sauce

prep time 15 minutes   cook time 20 minutes   serves 4

2 tablespoons olive oil

4 x 200g breast fillets

3 shallots (75g), chopped finely

1 clove garlic, crushed

½ cup (125ml) dry white wine

½ cup (125ml) chicken stock

2 tablespoons honey

2 teaspoons dijon mustard

½ cup (60g) roasted pecans,
  chopped coarsely

100g mesclun

1 tablespoon lemon juice

2 small pears (360g), sliced thinly

1   Heat half the oil in large frying pan; cook chicken, uncovered, until cooked through. Remove from pan; cover to keep warm.

2   Cook shallot and garlic in same heated pan, stirring, until onion softens. Add wine; bring to a boil. Reduce heat; simmer, uncovered, until liquid is reduced by half. Add stock, honey and mustard; cook, stirring, about 5 minutes or until liquid is reduced by half. Remove from heat; stir in nuts.

3   Combine mesclun with combined lemon juice and remaining oil in medium bowl. Cut chicken in half crossways; drizzle with sauce. Serve chicken with mesclun and pear.

per serving 7.2g total fat (1.3g saturated fat); 560kJ (134 cal); 5.1g carbohydrate; 10.6g protein; 1g fibre

creamy leek and chicken pies

prep time 5 minutes   cook time 30 minutes   serves 4

1 tablespoon olive oil
800g breast fillets, chopped coarsely
2 rindless bacon rashers (130g), sliced thinly
1 small leek (200g), trimmed, sliced thinly
½ cup (125ml) dry white wine
1 sheet ready-rolled puff pastry
20g butter
1 tablespoon plain flour
300ml cream
½ cup (125ml) milk
1 egg, beaten lightly

1   Preheat oven to 200°C/180°C fan-forced. Grease four 1¼-cup (310ml) ovenproof dishes.
2   Heat oil in large frying pan; cook chicken, uncovered, until cooked through. Remove from pan; cover.
3   Meanwhile, cook bacon and leek in same heated pan, stirring, until leek softens. Add wine; cook, stirring, until liquid is reduced by half.
4   Quarter pastry sheet; cut circles from each quarter slightly larger than the top of the dishes.
5   Melt butter in medium saucepan; add flour; cook, stirring, until mixture thickens and bubbles. Gradually stir in cream and milk until mixture boils and thickens. Stir in chicken and leek mixture. Divide mixture among dishes; press pastry rounds over dishes, brush with egg. Cut a slit in each pastry top; bake about 20 minutes or until browned.
per serving 67.3g total fat (35.6g saturated fat); 3933kJ (941 cal); 22.1g carbohydrate; 57.4g protein; 1.4g fibre

spiced grilled chicken with tomato chilli sauce

prep time 10 minutes   cook time 25 minutes   serves 4

2 teaspoons olive oil
¼ cup (60ml) lemon juice
1 teaspoon ground cumin
2 teaspoons sweet paprika
8 x 125g thigh fillets
tomato chilli sauce
¼ cup (55g) firmly packed brown sugar
¼ cup (60ml) red wine vinegar
2 fresh long red chillies, chopped coarsely
4 large egg tomatoes (360g),
   chopped coarsely

1   Make tomato chilli sauce.
2   Meanwhile, combine oil, juice, spices and chicken in medium bowl. Cook chicken on heated oiled grill plate (or grill or barbecue) until cooked through. Serve chicken topped with sauce.
tomato chilli sauce Combine sugar and vinegar in medium saucepan; cook, stirring, over low heat, until sugar dissolves. Add chilli and tomato; bring to a boil. Reduce heat; simmer, uncovered, 15 minutes. Drain sauce over small bowl; reserve solids. Return liquid to pan; bring to a boil. Boil, uncovered, until liquid is reduced by half. Return tomato solids to pan; stir over heat until sauce is hot.
per serving 20.4g total fat (5.8g saturated fat); 1747kJ (418 cal); 10.8 carbohydrate; 47.6g protein; 1.1g fibre

roasted kumara, craisin, chicken and spinach salad

prep time 10 minutes   cook time 35 minutes   serves 4

1 large kumara (500g), cut into 2cm pieces

1 medium red onion (170g), cut into wedges

1 tablespoon maple syrup

1 tablespoon olive oil

600g breast fillets

80g baby spinach leaves

⅓ cup (45g) craisins

⅓ cup (50g) pine nuts

cranberry dressing

2 tablespoons olive oil

¼ cup (80g) whole berry cranberry
   sauce, warmed

1 tablespoon red wine vinegar

1 Preheat oven to 220°C/200°C fan-forced.

2 Combine kumara, onion, syrup and oil in large shallow baking dish; roast about 35 minutes or until vegetables are tender, stirring halfway through roasting time.

3 Meanwhile, make cranberry dressing.

4 Cook chicken in heated oiled medium frying pan until cooked through. Remove from pan; slice thickly.

5 Combine kumara mixture, half the dressing, chicken, spinach, craisins and nuts in medium bowl. Divide salad among serving plates; drizzle with remaining dressing.

cranberry dressing Whisk ingredients in small jug to combine.

per serving 30.9g total fat (5g saturated fat); 2449kJ (586 cal); 37.7g carbohydrate; 37.2g protein; 4.3g fibre

Each of these recipes serves 4, and can be on the table in 30 minutes or less.

mexican-style chicken with salsa

Combine four 200g breast fillets with 35g packet taco seasoning mix in medium bowl. Cook chicken in heated oiled large frying pan until browned both sides and cooked through. Meanwhile, combine 2 coarsely chopped small avocados, 1 finely chopped medium egg tomato, ½ finely chopped small red onion, 1 finely chopped small red thai chilli and 1 tablespoon lime juice. Serve chicken with salsa. Goes well with warmed corn tortillas or grilled fresh corn cobs.

chicken masala with coconut raita

Combine four 200g breast fillets with 1 tablespoon vegetable oil and ¼ cup tikka masala paste in medium bowl. Cook chicken in heated oiled large frying pan until browned both sides and cooked through. Meanwhile, make raita by combining ⅓ cup flaked coconut, ¾ cup greek-style yogurt, 1 teaspoon finely grated lime rind and 1 tablespoon lime juice in small bowl. Serve chicken topped with raita. Goes well with steamed basmati rice and pappadums.

pan-fried chicken with chilli butter

Combine 60g softened butter, ½ teaspoon dried chilli flakes, 1 tablespoon coarsely chopped drained semi-dried tomatoes in oil and 1 tablespoon coarsely chopped roasted pine nuts in small bowl. Place mixture on piece of plastic wrap, shape into rectangular block, wrap tightly; freeze. Cook four 200g thigh fillets in heated oiled large frying pan until browned both sides and cooked through. Slice butter; serve on chicken. Goes well with roasted potato wedges.

chicken with garlic hoisin sauce

Cook four 200g thigh fillets in heated oiled large frying pan until cooked through; slice thickly. Meanwhile, combine 2 teaspoons white sugar, 1 tablespoon rice vinegar and ¼ cup water in small saucepan; stir over low heat until sugar dissolves. Stir in ¼ cup hoisin sauce and 1 clove crushed garlic; bring to a boil then remove from heat. Top chicken with sauce then sprinkle with 2 finely sliced green onions. Goes well with steamed jasmine rice.

thai red chicken curry & coriander

Preheat oven to 200°C/180°C fan-forced. Blend or process ½ cup roasted unsalted peanuts, 1 tablespoon red curry paste, 2 teaspoons kecap manis, ⅓ cup fresh coriander leaves and 60ml coconut milk; combine half the paste mixture with four 200g breast fillets in medium bowl. Cook chicken in heated oiled large frying pan until browned both sides; place on oven tray, top with remaining paste. Roast in oven about 15 minutes or until cooked through; sprinkle with coriander. Goes well with steamed jasmine rice.

chicken with prosciutto & capers

Wrap one slice of prosciutto tightly around each of four 200g breast fillets. Cook chicken in heated oiled large frying pan until cooked through; remove from pan, cover to keep warm. Melt 60g butter in same pan; add 2 tablespoons rinsed drained baby capers, 1 crushed garlic clove, 1 tablespoon finely chopped fresh basil and 1 tablespoon finely chopped fresh flat-leaf parsley, cook until herbs just wilt. Serve chicken with warm herb sauce. Goes well with penne napolitana.

dukkah-crumbed chicken

Combine eight 125g thigh fillets with 2 lightly beaten eggs in medium bowl. Combine ¼ cup dukkah spice mixture and ½ cup packaged breadcrumbs in shallow medium bowl. Coat chicken pieces with dukkah mixture. Heat 1 tablespoon olive oil in large frying pan; cook chicken until browned both sides and cooked through. Goes well with warmed pitta bread, hummus and either tabbouleh or fattoush salad.

roasted chicken with thyme butter

Preheat oven to 200°C/180°C fan-forced. Combine 60g softened butter, 2 crushed garlic cloves and 2 teaspoons finely chopped fresh thyme in small bowl. Loosen the skin on four 200g breast fillets; push thyme butter between skin and flesh. Cook chicken in heated oiled large frying pan until browned both sides then place on oven tray; roast in oven about 15 minutes or until cooked through. Goes well with mashed potato.

Fish fillets

If you're looking for food that's good for the heart and mind, fish should be your first pick. We've used salmon, ocean trout and various firm white fish fillets, however, feel free to use whatever fish takes your fancy.

salt and sichuan pepper salmon with wasabi mayonnaise

prep time 10 minutes cook time 15 minutes serves 4

2 teaspoons sea salt
2 teaspoons sichuan pepper
¼ cup (60ml) vegetable oil
4 x 200g salmon fillets, skin on
½ cup (150g) mayonnaise
2 teaspoons wasabi paste
1 teaspoon finely chopped fresh coriander
1 teaspoon lime juice

1 Using mortar and pestle or pepper grinder, grind salt and pepper until fine. Combine pepper mixture, half the oil and fish in large bowl, cover; stand 5 minutes.

2 Meanwhile, combine mayonnaise, wasabi, coriander and juice in small bowl.

3 Heat remaining oil in large frying pan; cook fish, skin-side down, until skin crisps. Turn fish; cook, uncovered, until cooked as desired. Serve fish with wasabi mayonnaise and watercress, if desired.

per serving 40.1g total fat (6.3g saturated fat); 2278kJ (545 cal); 7.5g carbohydrate; 39.4 protein; 0.2g fibre

ginger and kaffir lime perch parcels

prep time 5 minutes cook time 15 minutes serves 4

4 x 180g ocean perch fillets
3 green onions, sliced thinly
5cm piece fresh ginger (25g), sliced thinly
4 fresh kaffir lime leaves, shredded finely
2 teaspoons sesame oil

1 Preheat oven to 180°C/160°C fan-forced.
2 Place each fillet on large square of oiled foil or baking paper; top each with onion, ginger and lime leaves, drizzle with oil. Gather corners together; fold to enclose.
3 Place parcels on oven trays; cook about 15 minutes or until fish is cooked through.
4 Remove fish from parcel, discard topping from fish. Serve with wedges of lime and steamed jasmine rice, if desired.

per serving 3.4g total fat (0.5g saturated fat); 648kJ (155 cal); 6.3g carbohydrate; 30.4g protein; 0.2g fibre

chilli and lemon crumbed john dory

prep time 10 minutes cook time 20 minutes serves 4

2 cups (140g) stale breadcrumbs
2 fresh long red chillies, sliced thinly
1 clove garlic, crushed
1 tablespoon finely grated lemon rind
60g butter, melted
4 x 200g john dory fillets
1 tablespoon lemon juice
coconut rice
1¾ cups (350g) white long-grain rice
1¼ cups (310ml) water
400ml can coconut cream
1 teaspoon white sugar

1 Make coconut rice.
2 Preheat oven to 200°C/180°C fan-forced.
3 Meanwhile, combine breadcrumbs, chilli, garlic, rind and butter in medium bowl.
4 Place fish on oiled oven tray; pat crumb mixture onto fish, drizzle with juice. Cook, uncovered, about 15 minutes or until fish is cooked through. Serve fish with coconut rice and wedges of lemon, if desired.
coconut rice Rinse rice under water until water runs clear; drain. Combine rice with remaining ingredients in medium heavy-based saucepan; bring to a boil, stirring occasionally. Reduce heat; simmer, covered tightly, about 15 minutes or until rice is tender. Remove from heat; stand, covered, 5 minutes.

per serving 36.8g total fat (27.2g saturated fat); 3921kJ (938 cal); 98.3g carbohydrate; 50.6g protein; 4.5g fibre

spice-rubbed trout with cauliflower puree

prep time 15 minutes cook time 30 minutes serves 4

1 teaspoon ground cumin
1 teaspoon fennel seeds
½ teaspoon sweet paprika
1 clove garlic, quartered
1 teaspoon coarsely grated lemon rind
1 tablespoon olive oil
4 x 200g ocean trout fillets, skin on
800g cauliflower, chopped coarsely
30g butter
¼ cup (60ml) cream
30g butter, extra
2 tablespoons lemon juice

1 Dry-fry spices in small frying pan, stirring, until fragrant. Using mortar and pestle, grind spice mixture, garlic and rind until crushed.
2 Combine spice mixture, oil and fish in medium bowl. Cook fish in heated oiled large frying pan until cooked through. Remove from pan; cover to keep warm.
3 Meanwhile, boil, steam or microwave cauliflower until tender; drain. Mash cauliflower with butter and cream in large bowl until smooth. Cover to keep warm.
4 Melt extra butter in small saucepan; stir over low heat about 3 minutes or until browned lightly. Remove from heat; stir in juice.
5 Serve trout with cauliflower puree and browned butter.
per serving 31.4g total fat (14.8g saturated fat); 2019kJ (483 cal); 5.1g carbohydrate; 43.7g protein; 3.8g fibre

blue-eye with chunky tomato, anchovy and caper sauce

prep time 15 minutes cook time 15 minutes serves 4

1 tablespoon olive oil

4 x 200g blue-eye fillets

1 medium brown onion (150g),
   chopped finely

2 cloves garlic, crushed

4 medium tomatoes (600g), peeled,
   seeded, chopped coarsely

4 anchovy fillets, drained, chopped finely

1 tablespoon rinsed capers, drained

1 teaspoon white sugar

¼ cup coarsely chopped fresh
   flat-leaf parsley

1 Heat half the oil in large frying pan; cook fish, uncovered, until cooked as desired.

2 Meanwhile, heat remaining oil in small saucepan; cook onion and garlic, stirring, until onion softens. Add tomato; cook, stirring, 1 minute. Remove from heat; stir in anchovy, capers, sugar and parsley. Serve fish with sauce, and lemon wedges, if desired.

per serving 7.1g total fat (1.1g saturated fat); 1099kJ (263 cal); 6.4g carbohydrate; 41.8g protein; 2.8g fibre

tandoori blue-eye with green chilli rice

prep time 10 minutes cook time 25 minutes serves 4

2 tablespoons tandoori paste

400ml can coconut milk

4 x 200g blue-eye fillets

2 teaspoons vegetable oil

2 large carrots (360g), cut into matchsticks

1 medium red onion (170g), sliced thinly

green chilli rice

1 cup (200g) jasmine rice

⅔ cup (160ml) water

2 long green chillies, sliced thinly

1 teaspoon finely grated lime rind

1 Combine paste, ⅓ cup of the coconut milk and fish in large bowl; stand 5 minutes.

2 Meanwhile, make green chilli rice.

3 Heat oil in large frying pan; cook carrot and onion, stirring, about 2 minutes. Place fish mixture on top of vegetables; cook, covered, 10 minutes. Uncover; cook about 5 minutes or until fish is cooked through. Serve fish with vegetables and rice, and pappadums, if desired.

green chilli rice Rinse rice under cold water until water runs clear; drain. Combine rice with water, chilli, rind and remaining coconut milk in medium heavy-based saucepan; bring to a boil, stirring occasionally. Reduce heat; simmer, covered tightly, about 15 minutes or until rice is tender. Remove from heat; stand, covered, 5 minutes.

per serving 28.4g total fat (19.1g saturated fat); 2671kJ (639 cal); 50.7g carbohydrate; 42.1g protein; 6.2g fibre

ocean trout with lime and lemon grass hollandaise

prep time 20 minutes   cook time 10 minutes   serves 4

10cm stick fresh lemon grass (20g),
    chopped finely
3 fresh kaffir lime leaves, shredded thinly
1 tablespoon finely grated lime rind
⅓ cup (80ml) lime juice
3 egg yolks
200g unsalted butter, melted
3 fresh kaffir lime leaves, chopped finely
4 x 200g ocean trout fillets

1   To make lime and lemon grass hollandaise, combine lemon grass, shredded lime leaves, rind and juice in small saucepan; bring to a boil. Reduce heat; simmer, uncovered, until liquid reduces to 1 tablespoon. Strain through fine sieve into medium heatproof bowl; cool 10 minutes. Discard solids in sieve.

2   Add egg yolks to juice mixture in bowl; set bowl over medium saucepan of simmering water, do not allow water to touch base of bowl. Whisk mixture over heat until thickened.

3   Remove bowl from heat; gradually add melted butter in thin, steady stream, whisking constantly until sauce has thickened. (If sauce is too thick, a tablespoon of hot water can be added.) Stir in finely chopped lime leaves.

4   Meanwhile, cook fish in heated oiled large frying pan until cooked as desired. Serve with hollandaise.

per serving 52.9g total fat (30.1g saturated fat); 2675kJ (640 cal); 0.7g carbohydrate; 41.6g protein; 0.1g fibre

steamed salmon with burnt orange sauce

prep time 10 minutes cook time 25 minutes serves 4

½ cup (110g) caster sugar
⅓ cup (80ml) water
1 teaspoon finely grated orange rind
¼ cup (60ml) orange juice
1 tablespoon olive oil
1 tablespoon rice wine vinegar
4 x 200g salmon fillets
350g watercress, trimmed

1 Combine sugar and the water in small saucepan; stir, without boiling, until sugar dissolves, bring to a boil. Reduce heat; simmer, uncovered, without stirring, until mixture is a light caramel colour.

2 Remove pan from heat; allow bubbles to subside. Carefully stir in rind and juice; return pan to low heat. Stir until any pieces of caramel melt. Remove pan from heat; stir in oil and vinegar.

3 Meanwhile, place fish in large bamboo steamer set over large saucepan of simmering water; steam, covered, 15 minutes. Serve fish with watercress, drizzled with sauce.

per serving 19.1g total fat (3.8g saturated fat); 1940kJ (464 cal); 29.4g carbohydrate; 41.6g protein; 3.4g fibre

beer-battered fish with lemon mayonnaise

prep time **10 minutes** cook time **20 minutes** serves **4**

You can use any firm white fish fillet, such as perch, ling or blue-eye, for this recipe.

⅔ cup (200g) mayonnaise
2 teaspoons finely grated lemon rind
¼ teaspoon cracked black pepper
1 teaspoon lemon juice
¾ cup (110g) self-raising flour
¾ cup (110g) plain flour
1 teaspoon five-spice powder
1 egg
1½ cups (375ml) beer
vegetable oil, for deep-frying
600g white fish fillets

1 Combine mayonnaise, rind, pepper and juice in small bowl.
2 Whisk flours, five-spice, egg and beer in medium bowl until smooth.
3 Heat oil in large saucepan. Dip fish in batter; deep-fry fish, in batches, until cooked through. Serve with mayonnaise, and lemon wedges, if desired.
per serving 29.7g total fat (4.4g saturated fat); 2746kJ (657 cal); 51.2g carbohydrate; 38.7g protein; 2.4g fibre

polenta-crumbed fish with rocket sauce

prep time 15 minutes cook time 15 minutes serves 4

You can use any firm white fish fillet, such as perch, ling or blue-eye, for this recipe.

⅔ cup (200g) mayonnaise
50g baby rocket leaves
1 clove garlic, crushed
600g white fish fillets
1 cup (170g) polenta
2 tablespoons finely chopped
  fresh flat-leaf parsley
2 teaspoons finely grated lemon rind
2 egg whites
vegetable oil, for shallow-frying

1 Blend or process mayonnaise, rocket and garlic until sauce is smooth.
2 Cut fish into 2cm strips. Combine polenta, parsley and rind in shallow medium bowl. Whisk egg whites lightly in another shallow medium bowl. Dip fish in egg white then coat in polenta mixture.
3 Heat oil in large frying pan; shallow-fry fish, in batches, until cooked through. Serve fish with sauce.

per serving 28.6g total fat (4g saturated fat); 2370kJ (567 cal); 39.7g carbohydrate; 36.7g protein; 2g fibre

fish pie with caper rösti topping

prep time 10 minutes   cook time 25 minutes   serves 4

600g ling fillets, chopped coarsely

100g uncooked small prawns,
   shelled, deveined

¼ cup (35g) plain flour

25g butter

½ cup (120g) sour cream

½ cup (60g) frozen peas

¼ cup coarsely chopped fresh dill

caper rösti topping

500g russet burbank potatoes, peeled
   grated coarsely

2 tablespoons rinsed baby capers, drained

25g butter, melted

1 Make caper rösti topping.

2 Coat seafood in flour; shake off excess. Heat butter in large frying pan; cook seafood, in batches, 3 minutes. Return seafood to pan with sour cream, peas and dill; cook, stirring occasionally, about 5 minutes or until seafood is cooked through.

3 Preheat grill. Spread seafood into shallow 2.5-litre (10-cup) baking dish; top with caper rösti mixture. Grill about 10 minutes or until topping is tender and golden brown.

caper rösti topping Squeeze excess moisture from potato; combine with capers and butter in medium bowl.

per serving 23.4g total fat (14.8g saturated fat); 1910kJ (457 cal); 23g carbohydrate; 37.3g protein; 3g fibre

Each of these recipes serves 4, and can be on the table in 30 minutes or less.

cantonese ling braise

Cook 1 thinly sliced medium red capsicum, 1 thinly sliced medium brown onion and 1 thinly sliced fresh long red chilli in heated oiled large frying pan until softened. Add ½ cup water, a grated 2cm piece fresh ginger, 1 tablespoon black bean sauce and 1 teaspoon caster sugar; bring to a boil. Place four 200g ling fillets on vegetable mixture in pan, reduce heat; simmer, covered, about 5 minutes or until fish is cooked through. Serve fish topped with sauce. Goes well with steamed asian green vegetables.

bream in macadamia butter

Dry-fry ½ cup macadamias in large frying pan over low heat, shaking pan constantly, until fragrant; remove from heat. When cool enough to handle, chop nuts coarsely. Melt 80g butter in same pan; cook nuts and ⅓ cup finely chopped fresh coriander, stirring, for 1 minute. Add four 200g bream fillets to pan; cook, turning halfway through cooking, until cooked through. Serve fish drizzled with butter. Goes well with steamed baby green beans.

pan-fried blue-eye with pepitas

Blend or process ¼ cup roasted pepitas, 1 quartered garlic clove, ⅓ cup sour cream and 1 tablespoon lemon juice until mixture is almost smooth. Cook four 200g blue-eye fillets in heated oiled large frying pan until cooked as desired. Meanwhile, heat four small flour tortillas according to manufacturer's instructions. Serve each fillet of fish, drizzled with pepita cream, on a tortilla. Goes well with spicy avocado and tomato salsa.

salmon green curry

Rub 2 tablespoons green curry paste into four 200g salmon fillets in medium bowl. Cook fish in heated oiled large frying pan until cooked as desired. Meanwhile, combine ⅓ cup coarsely chopped roasted unsalted cashews, ⅓ cup coarsely chopped fresh coriander, 1 tablespoon vegetable oil, 1 teaspoon finely grated lime rind and 1 tablespoon lime juice in small bowl. Serve fish topped with herb and nut mixture. Goes well with steamed jasmine rice.

cajun kingfish

Combine 2 teaspoons each sweet paprika, ground cumin, ground coriander, mustard powder and fennel seeds with ¼ teaspoon cayenne pepper in small bowl. Rub mixture into four 200g kingfish fillets; cook fish in heated oiled large frying pan until cooked as desired, remove from pan. Heat 2 teaspoons olive oil in same cleaned pan; cook 1 sliced small red onion and 1 chopped large tomato, until soft. Add 420g can rinsed, drained kidney beans; stir until hot, serve with fish. Goes well with coleslaw.

blue-eye with ginger & orange

Combine 2 tablespoons orange marmalade, 1 tablespoon kecap manis, 1 finely chopped fresh small thai red chilli and 3cm piece grated ginger in small bowl. Cook four 200g blue-eye fillets in heated oiled large frying pan until browned both sides. Pour marmalade mixture over fish; cook, spooning sauce over fish until fish is cooked as desired. Goes well with fresh lime slices and fresh rice noodles stir-fried with grated zucchini and cabbage.

ocean trout with anchovy

Heat 60g butter in large frying pan; add 2 crushed garlic cloves, 4 finely chopped drained anchovy fillets, 2 tablespoons flaked almonds and four 200g ocean trout fillets to pan; cook, covered, about 5 minutes or until cooked as desired. Remove fish from pan; stir 2 tablespoons lemon juice and ¼ cup finely chopped fresh flat-leaf parsley into anchovy butter sauce. Serve fish drizzled with sauce. Goes well with broccolini steamed with lemon juice.

grilled flathead with tzatziki

Preheat grill. Combine ½ cup greek-style yogurt, 1 finely chopped lebanese cucumber, ¼ teaspoon ground cumin and 1 tablespoon finely chopped fresh mint in small bowl, cover tzatziki; refrigerate. Toss 250g halved cherry tomatoes with 1 tablespoon olive oil on oven tray. Rub 2 teaspoons ground cumin into eight 100g flathead fillets; place fish on tray with tomato, spread fish with ⅓ cup mint jelly. Grill fish and tomato about 5 minutes or until fish is cooked through; serve with tzatziki. Goes well with baked potato wedges.

Beef fillets

A fantastic source of iron and oh-so-quick to cook. After cooking, be sure to let the beef stand for at least 5 minutes before slicing it; by doing this, you allow the delicious juices to settle, ensuring that the beef is tender and easy to cut.

spicy beef and bean salad

prep time 10 minutes   cook time 20 minutes   serves 4

¼ cup (60ml) olive oil

35g packet taco seasoning mix

600g piece eye fillet

2 tablespoons lime juice

1 clove garlic, crushed

420g can four-bean mix, rinsed, drained

310g can corn kernels, rinsed, drained

2 lebanese cucumbers (260g),
   chopped finely

1 small red onion (100g), chopped finely

1 large red capsicum (350g), chopped finely

½ cup coarsely chopped fresh coriander

1 fresh long red chilli, chopped finely

1 Combine 1 tablespoon of the oil, seasoning and beef in medium bowl. Cook beef on heated grill plate (or grill or barbecue) until cooked as desired. Cover, stand 5 minutes then slice thinly.

2 Meanwhile, whisk remaining oil, juice and garlic in large bowl. Add remaining ingredients; toss gently to combine. Serve beef with salad; sprinkle with coriander, if desired.

per serving 22.2g total fat (5.2g saturated fat); 2111kJ (505 cal); 30.9g carbohydrate; 40.4g protein; 9.3g fibre

tomato, pesto and olive pasta
with sliced fillet

prep time 15 minutes cook time 20 minutes serves 6

Farfalle, the Italian pasta known in English as butterflies or bow ties, is good to use in dishes such as this because they help hold the other ingredients. You can replace farfalle with penne or spirals, if you prefer.

⅓ cup (80ml) olive oil
600g piece eye fillet
250g cherry tomatoes, halved
500g farfalle
⅔ cup (80g) seeded black olives
¼ cup (65g) basil pesto
2 teaspoons finely grated lemon rind
1 cup loosely packed fresh basil leaves, torn
1 cup (200g) ricotta cheese, crumbled

1 Heat 1 tablespoon of the oil in large frying pan; cook beef until cooked as desired. Remove from pan; cover to keep warm. Add tomato to same pan; cook, stirring occasionally, until just softened. Slice beef thickly.
2 Meanwhile, cook pasta in large saucepan of boiling water until just tender; drain.
3 Combine pasta and tomato in large bowl with remaining oil, olives, pesto, rind and basil. Serve topped with beef and cheese.
per serving 28.7g total fat (7.5g saturated fat); 2721kJ (651 cal); 60.8g carbohydrate; 35.1g protein; 4g fibre

char-grilled steak and vegetables
with baba ghanoush

prep time 15 minutes cook time 20 minutes serves 4

3 cloves garlic, crushed
2 tablespoons olive oil
2 teaspoons finely grated lemon rind
4 x 150g eye fillet steaks
2 medium red capsicums (400g),
    sliced thickly
2 large zucchini (300g), halved crossways,
    sliced thinly lengthways
½ cup (120g) baba ghanoush
⅓ cup loosely packed fresh mint leaves

1 Combine garlic, oil, rind, beef, capsicum and zucchini in large bowl. Cook beef and vegetables on heated grill plate (or grill or barbecue), in batches, until beef is cooked as desired and vegetables are tender.
2 Divide vegetables among serving plates, top with beef. Serve with baba ghanoush and mint.
per serving 17.3g total fat (4.6g saturated fat); 1354kJ (324 cal); 5.9g carbohydrate; 34.2g protein; 3.6g fibre

pho bo

prep time 10 minutes cook time 15 minutes serves 4

Pho, the Vietnamese word for rice noodles, is a breakfast staple throughout Vietnam. While it's adored by those of us introduced to it, we tend to prefer it for lunch or dinner. Bo means beef in Vietnam, where it is usually sliced extremely thinly and served raw, then cooked once it's submerged in the hot broth. You need a large bunch of coriander for this recipe, with roots and stems intact.

1 litre (4 cups) water

1 litre (4 cups) beef stock

8cm piece fresh ginger (40g), sliced thinly

1 tablespoon fish sauce

1 tablespoon lime juice

2 cloves garlic, quartered

1/3 cup coarsely chopped fresh coriander root and stem mixture

1 star anise

500g piece eye fillet, sliced thinly

375g dried rice stick noodles

8 green onions, sliced thinly

2 cups (160g) bean sprouts

1/3 cup loosely packed vietnamese mint leaves

1/3 cup loosely packed fresh coriander leaves

2 fresh small red thai chillies, chopped finely

2 lemons, cut into wedges

1 Combine the water, stock, ginger, sauce, juice, garlic, coriander mixture and star anise in large saucepan; bring to a boil. Reduce heat; simmer, uncovered, 10 minutes.

2 Strain broth through muslin-lined sieve into large heatproof bowl; discard solids. Return broth to pan, add beef; return to a boil. Reduce heat; simmer, uncovered, about 3 minutes or until beef is cooked as desired.

3 Meanwhile, place noodles in large heatproof bowl, cover with boiling water; stand until tender, drain.

4 Divide noodles, onion and sprouts among serving bowls; ladle hot broth into bowls. Serve with separate bowls of herbs, chilli and lemon, so each person can add what they wish to their bowl.

per serving 7.1g total fat (2.9g saturated fat); 1271kJ (304 cal); 24.3g carbohydrate; 33.5g protein; 3g fibre

steak sandwich with tarragon and tomato salsa

prep time 15 minutes cook time 15 minutes serves 4

Use ciabatta, foccacia or even individual pide (turkish bread) for this recipe.

You need 80g watercress to get the amount of trimmed watercress required for this recipe.

4 x 125g scotch fillet steaks

2 cloves garlic, crushed

1 tablespoon dijon mustard

1 tablespoon olive oil

8 thick slices bread (320g)

⅓ cup (100g) mayonnaise

40g trimmed watercress

tarragon and tomato salsa

2 cloves garlic, crushed

3 large egg tomatoes (270g), quartered, sliced thinly

½ small red onion (50g), sliced thinly

1 tablespoon finely chopped fresh tarragon

1 Combine beef, garlic, mustard and half the oil in medium bowl.

2 Make tarragon and tomato salsa.

3 Cook beef on heated grill plate (or grill or barbecue) until cooked as desired. Remove from heat, cover; stand 5 minutes.

4 Meanwhile, brush both sides of bread with remaining oil; toast on same grill. Spread one side of each slice with mayonnaise; sandwich watercress, beef and salsa between slices.

tarragon and tomato salsa Combine ingredients in medium bowl.

per serving 21.6g total fat (4.6g saturated fat); 2161kJ (517 cal); 43.3g carbohydrate; 35g protein; 4.2g fibre

hokkien mee

prep time 15 minutes cook time 15 minutes serves 4

Hokkien, also known as stir-fry noodles, are fresh chinese wheat noodles that resemble thick, yellow-brown spaghetti. Hokkien mee is a flavourful fried noodle, vegetable and beef dish that has become synonymous with fried noodles and is eaten all over the world wherever noodle shops are found.

450g hokkien noodles

1 tablespoon peanut oil

600g piece eye fillet, sliced thinly

1 medium brown onion (150g), sliced thinly

2 cloves garlic, crushed

1 medium red capsicum (200g), sliced thinly

115g baby corn, halved lengthways

150g snow peas, trimmed,
  halved diagonally

2 baby buk choy (300g), chopped coarsely

¼ cup (60ml) char siu sauce

1 tablespoon dark soy sauce

¼ cup (60ml) chicken stock

1 Place noodles in medium heatproof bowl, cover with boiling water; separate with fork, drain.

2 Heat half the oil in wok; stir-fry beef, in batches, until browned.

3 Heat remaining oil in wok; stir-fry onion, garlic and capsicum until tender.

4 Return beef to wok with noodles, corn, snow peas, buk choy, sauces and stock; stir-fry until vegetables are tender and beef is cooked as desired.

per serving 10.8g total fat (4.6g saturated fat); 1129kJ (270 cal); 25.2g carbohydrate; 25.7g protein; 4.4g fibre

beef and zucchini red curry

prep time 10 minutes   cook time 25 minutes   serves 4

1 tablespoon peanut oil
4 x 200g scotch fillet steaks
¼ cup (75g) red curry paste
225g can bamboo shoots, rinsed, drained
400ml can coconut milk
¼ cup (60ml) water
1 tablespoon fish sauce
1 tablespoon lime juice
2 fresh kaffir lime leaves, shredded finely
4 large zucchini (600g), sliced thickly
⅓ cup firmly packed thai basil leaves

1 Heat oil in large frying pan; cook beef until cooked as desired. Remove from pan; stand 5 minutes. Slice thickly; cover to keep warm.
2 Meanwhile, cook paste in same pan, stirring, until fragrant. Add bamboo shoots, coconut milk, the water, sauce, juice and lime leaves; simmer, uncovered, 10 minutes. Add zucchini; simmer, uncovered, until tender. Stir through sliced beef.
3 Serve curry sprinkled with basil and accompanied with steamed jasmine rice, if desired.

per serving 41.2g total fat (23.8g saturated fat); 2529kJ (605 cal); 8.4g carbohydrate; 47.3g protein; 6.9g fibre

grilled mixed mushrooms and steak with creamy polenta

prep time 15 minutes cook time 20 minutes serves 4

3 large flat mushrooms (240g), sliced thickly

200g swiss brown mushrooms, halved

4 x 200g scotch fillet steaks

2 cups (500ml) water

2½ cups (625ml) milk

1 cup (170g) polenta

½ cup (40g) finely grated parmesan cheese

100g baby spinach leaves

2 tablespoons balsamic vinegar

1 Cook mushrooms and beef on heated oiled grill plate (or grill or barbecue); cover both separately to keep warm.

2 Meanwhile, combine the water and milk in large saucepan, bring to a boil; gradually stir in polenta. Reduce heat; cook, stirring, about 10 minutes or until polenta thickens. Remove from heat; stir in cheese and spinach.

3 Serve beef, drizzled with vinegar, with polenta and mushrooms.

per serving 20.2g total fat (10.4g saturated fat); 2424kJ (580 cal); 37.3g carbohydrate; 58.9g protein; 4.7g fibre

scotch fillet with pepper thyme sauce

prep time 10 minutes cook time 15 minutes serves 4

1 tablespoon olive oil

4 x 200g scotch fillet steaks

1 trimmed celery stalk (100g), chopped finely

1 medium brown onion (150g), chopped finely

½ cup (125ml) dry white wine

300ml cream

1 tablespoon mixed peppercorns, crushed

1 tablespoon coarsely chopped fresh thyme

1 Heat half the oil in large frying pan; cook beef until cooked as desired. Remove from pan; cover to keep warm.

2 Heat remaining oil in same pan; cook celery and onion, stirring, until vegetables soften. Add wine; stir until liquid is reduced by half. Add cream and peppercorns; bring to a boil. Reduce heat; simmer, uncovered, stirring occasionally, about 5 minutes or until sauce thickens slightly. Remove from heat; stir in thyme.

3 Serve beef drizzled with sauce, and accompanied with chunky chips, if desired.

per serving 46.7g total fat (26.3g saturated fat); 2658kJ (636 cal); 5g carbohydrate; 44.2g protein; 1.4g fibre

fajitas with guacamole and salsa cruda

prep time **25 minutes** cook time **15 minutes** serves **4**

3 cloves garlic, crushed

¼ cup (60ml) lemon juice

2 teaspoons ground cumin

1 tablespoon olive oil

600g piece eye fillet, sliced thinly

1 large red capsicum (350g), sliced thinly

1 large green capsicum (350g), sliced thinly

1 medium yellow capsicum (200g),
    sliced thinly

1 large red onion (300g), sliced thinly

8 large flour tortillas

guacamole

1 large avocado (320g), mashed roughly

¼ cup finely chopped fresh coriander

1 tablespoon lime juice

1 small white onion (80g), chopped finely

salsa cruda

2 medium tomatoes (300g), seeded,
    chopped finely

1 fresh long red chilli, chopped finely

½ cup coarsely chopped fresh coriander

1 small white onion (80g), chopped finely

1 tablespoon lime juice

1 Combine garlic, juice, cumin, oil and beef in large bowl, cover; refrigerate.

2 Make guacamole. Make salsa cruda.

3 Cook beef, in batches, in heated oiled large frying pan until cooked as desired. Remove from pan; cover to keep warm.

4 Cook capsicum and onion in same pan until softened. Return beef to pan; stir until heated through.

5 Meanwhile, warm tortillas according to manufacturer's instructions.

6 Divide beef mixture among serving plates; serve with tortillas, guacamole and salsa.

guacamole Combine ingredients in small bowl.

salsa cruda Combine ingredients in small bowl.

per serving 31.5g total fat (7.6g saturated fat); 3089kJ (739 cal); 62.7g carbohydrate; 46.2g protein; 8.9g fibre

smoky piquant steak and roasted beetroot salad

prep time 15 minutes cook time 25 minutes serves 4

4 x 200g scotch fillet steaks

2 teaspoons smoked paprika

2 tablespoons olive oil

2 tablespoons coarsely chopped
  fresh oregano

5 medium beetroots (1.5kg),
  cut into 1cm cubes

2 cloves garlic, crushed

2 tablespoons red wine vinegar

1 teaspoon white sugar

100g baby spinach leaves

1 Preheat oven to 180°C/160°C fan-forced.

2 Combine beef, paprika, half the oil and half the oregano in medium bowl. Cover; refrigerate.

3 Meanwhile, combine beetroot with garlic and remaining oil in large shallow baking dish. Roast about 20 minutes or until beetroot is tender.

4 Cook beef, in batches, in heated oiled large frying pan until cooked as desired. Remove from pan; stand 5 minutes. Slice thickly; cover to keep warm.

5 Meanwhile, whisk vinegar and sugar in large bowl; add sliced beef, beetroot, remaining oregano and spinach, toss to combine.

per serving 12.4g total fat (4.5g saturated fat); 1965kJ (470 cal); 32.9g carbohydrate; 49.6g protein; 12.6g fibre

saltimbocca

prep time 10 minutes cook time 25 minutes serves 4

Saltimbocca is a classic Italian dish that literally translates as "jump in the mouth", and it's one of the very few dishes that retains its Italian name on menus in countries all over the world – probably because the word so accurately describes the essence of the dish.

8 x 100g scotch fillet steaks

4 slices prosciutto (60g), halved crossways

8 fresh sage leaves

½ cup (40g) finely grated pecorino cheese

40g butter

1 cup (250ml) dry white wine

1 tablespoon coarsely chopped fresh sage

1 Place beef on board; using meat mallet, flatten slightly. Centre one piece prosciutto, one sage leaf and an eighth of the cheese on each piece of beef; fold in half, secure with a toothpick.

2 Melt half the butter in large frying pan; cook saltimbocca about 5 minutes or until cooked through. Remove from pan; cover to keep warm.

3 Pour wine into same pan; bring to a boil. Boil, uncovered, until liquid is reduced by half. Stir in remaining butter and chopped sage.

4 Serve saltimbocca, drizzled with sauce, with steamed baby green beans, if desired.

per serving 21.4g total fat (11.6g saturated fat); 1777kJ (425 cal); 0.3g carbohydrate; 47.5g protein; 0g fibre

honey-mustard beef with macadamia rice

prep time **5 minutes** cook time **35 minutes** serves **4**

Honeycup mustard is available from some supermarkets, delicatessens and butchers. If you prefer, you can simply combine dijon mustard with honey in the proportion of 1 tablespoon dijon to 2 tablespoons honey.

600g piece scotch fillet

⅓ cup (95g) honeycup mustard

¼ cup (60ml) cream

macadamia rice

20g butter

1 medium brown onion (150g), sliced thinly

1 clove garlic, crushed

2 teaspoons yellow mustard seeds

1 cup (200g) basmati rice

1 cup (125ml) chicken stock

1 cup (125ml) water

1 cup coarsely chopped fresh flat-leaf parsley

½ cup (70g) coarsely chopped roasted macadamias

1 Preheat oven to 240°C/220°C fan-forced.

2 Place beef in medium baking dish; brush all over with half the mustard. Roast about 35 minutes or until cooked as desired. Remove from oven; cover to keep warm.

3 Meanwhile, make macadamia rice.

4 Heat remaining mustard and cream in small saucepan.

5 Serve beef, drizzled with sauce, with macadamia rice.

macadamia rice Melt butter in medium saucepan; cook onion, garlic and seeds, stirring, until onion softens. Add rice; cook, stirring, 1 minute. Stir in stock and the water; bring to a boil. Reduce heat; simmer, covered, about 25 minutes or until rice is just tender. Remove from heat, fluff rice with fork, stir in parsley and nuts.

per serving 32.3g total fat (12.1g saturated fat); 2646kJ (633 cal); 44.6g carbohydrate; 38.9g protein; 3.8g fibre

steak with peppercorn and pepita rub

prep time 15 minutes cook time 15 minutes serves 4

1 clove garlic, quartered

1 tablespoon mixed peppercorns

½ teaspoon sea salt

1 tablespoon olive oil

⅓ cup (65g) roasted pepitas

4 x 200g scotch fillet steaks

25g butter

2 teaspoons red wine vinegar

1 tablespoon redcurrant jelly

420g can white beans, rinsed, drained

250g cherry tomatoes, halved

¼ cup fresh basil leaves

1 small radicchio (150g), trimmed

redcurrant dressing

¼ cup (60ml) olive oil

2 tablespoons red wine vinegar

1 tablespoon redcurrant jelly

1 Make redcurrant dressing.

2 Using mortar and pestle, crush garlic, peppercorns, salt, oil and 1 tablespoon of the pepitas to form a paste. Rub paste into beef.

3 Heat butter in large frying pan; cook beef until cooked as desired. Remove from pan; cover to keep warm. Add vinegar and jelly to pan; stir until combined.

4 Meanwhile, combine dressing, remaining pepitas, beans, tomato, basil and radicchio in large bowl.

5 Serve beef, drizzled with pan juices, with salad.

redcurrant dressing Place ingredients in screw-top jar; shake well.

per serving 41.3g total fat (11.3g saturated fat); 2784kJ (666 cal); 20.1g carbohydrate; 50.1g protein; 7.3g fibre

Each of these recipes serves 4, and can be on the table in 30 minutes or less.

steak & chilli tomato sauce

Cook four 200g scotch fillet steaks in heated oiled large frying pan until cooked as desired; cover to keep warm. Meanwhile, heat 2 teaspoons vegetable oil in medium saucepan; cook 1 finely chopped small brown onion and 1 crushed garlic clove, stirring, until onion softens. Add 3 finely chopped seeded medium tomatoes, 2 finely chopped fresh small red thai chillies and 2 teaspoons tomato paste; cook, stirring, 5 minutes. Serve steaks with sauce. Goes well with creamy polenta.

tex-mex grilled fillet

Cook four 200g scotch fillet steaks on heated oiled grill plate (or grill or barbecue) until cooked as desired; cover to keep warm. Meanwhile, combine 1 finely chopped medium red capsicum, 1 finely chopped medium yellow capsicum, 1 finely chopped medium green capsicum, 1 finely chopped fresh small red thai chilli, 1 tablespoon olive oil and 1 tablespoon lime juice in medium bowl. Toss salsa gently; serve with steaks. Goes well with grilled potato and kumara slices.

beef, beetroot & witlof salad

Cook 600g piece eye fillet on heated oiled grill plate (or grill or barbecue) until cooked as desired. Cover; stand 10 minutes. Meanwhile, whisk ¼ cup olive oil and 1 tablespoon wholegrain mustard in small jug. Cut beef into 1cm-thick slices. Place sliced beef in large bowl with leaves of 2 trimmed white witlof, ¾ cup roasted pecans and 450g can rinsed, drained baby beetroot. Toss salad gently; sprinkle with 120g crumbled soft goat cheese and drizzle with dressing.

herb-crumbed fillets

Cook four 200g scotch fillet steaks, uncovered, in heated oiled large frying pan until cooked as desired; place on oven tray. Meanwhile, combine 1¼ cups fresh breadcrumbs, 40g melted butter, 1 tablespoon wholegrain mustard, 1 tablespoon finely chopped fresh basil and 2 teaspoons finely chopped fresh rosemary in small bowl. Sprinkle breadcrumb mixture over top of steaks; brown lightly under preheated grill. Goes well with chunky potato chips or mashed potatoes.

steak with salsa verde

Cook four 200g scotch fillet steaks on heated oiled grill plate (or grill or barbecue) until cooked as desired. Cover; stand 5 minutes. Meanwhile, mix ¼ cup finely chopped fresh flat-leaf parsley, 2 tablespoons each finely chopped fresh dill and finely chopped fresh chives, 1 tablespoon rinsed drained baby capers, 1 crushed garlic clove, 2 tablespoons olive oil, 1 tablespoon lemon juice and 2 teaspoons wholegrain mustard in small bowl. Serve steaks topped with salsa verde. Goes well with sun-dried tomato risotto.

satay beef skewers

Mix 160ml can coconut cream, ¼ cup crunchy peanut butter, 1 crushed garlic clove, 1 finely chopped fresh small red thai chilli and 1 tablespoon each fish sauce and kecap manis in medium jug. Cut 800g piece eye fillet into 3cm dice; thread onto 8 pre-soaked bamboo skewers. Brush ½ cup of the satay sauce over beef. Cook on heated oiled grill plate (or grill or barbecue) until cooked as desired. Bring remaining satay sauce to a boil in small saucepan; drizzle over skewers to serve. Goes well with steamed rice.

steak sandwich revisited

Cook three 150g eye fillet steaks, uncovered, in heated oiled medium frying pan until cooked as desired. Cover; stand 5 minutes then slice thinly. Meanwhile, slice 2 small french bread sticks lengthways, do not cut all the way through; halve each stick crossways. Fill each of the 4 bread pieces with equal amounts of 40g trimmed watercress, sliced beef and combined 1 tablespoon horseradish cream and 1 tablespoon sour cream. Goes well with mixed lettuce and tomato salad.

scotch fillet in BBQ sauce

Combine 2 tablespoons brown sugar, 2 tablespoons barbecue sauce, 2 tablespoons tomato sauce, 2 teaspoons sweet smoked paprika and 1 tablespoon red wine vinegar in large bowl; place four 200g scotch fillet steaks in bowl, turn to coat all over in barbecue sauce mixture. Cook beef on heated oiled grill plate (or grill or barbecue) until cooked as desired. Cover; stand 5 minutes before serving. Goes well with grilled cobs of corn.

Lamb fillets

When you're pushed for time, why not give our lamb recipes a go; easy to prepare, this versatile meat marries well with many different foods. To enjoy lamb at its succulent best, cook it medium-rare.

lamb korma with cauliflower pulao

prep time 10 minutes   cook time 25 minutes   serves 4

The delicate use of strongly perfumed nutmeg, saffron and cardamom is quintessential to the flavour of a mild, creamy Indian korma.

800g backstraps
2 tablespoons korma paste
cauliflower pulao
25g butter
1 medium brown onion (150g), sliced thinly
1 clove garlic, crushed
½ teaspoon ground turmeric
1 teaspoon brown mustard seeds
1 cup (200g) basmati rice
1 cup (250ml) chicken stock
1 cup (250ml) water
½ small cauliflower (500g), cut into florets
½ cup coarsely chopped fresh coriander

1 Combine lamb and paste in medium bowl.
2 Make cauliflower pulao.
3 Cook lamb, uncovered, in heated oiled large frying pan until cooked as desired. Cover; stand 5 minutes then slice thickly.
4 Serve lamb with pulao, and yogurt and lemon wedges, if desired.
cauliflower pulao Melt butter in large frying pan; cook onion, garlic, turmeric and seeds, stirring, until onion softens. Add rice; cook, stirring, 1 minute. Stir in stock and the water; bring to a boil. Reduce heat; simmer, covered, 10 minutes. Stir cauliflower through rice, cover; cook about 10 minutes or until rice is tender. Remove from heat; fluff pulao with fork, stir through coriander.
per serving 16.7g total fat (7.1g saturated fat); 2261kJ (541 cal); 45.6g carbohydrate; 49.1g protein; 4.8g fibre

souvlaki with tomato, almond and mint salad

prep time 20 minutes cook time 15 minutes serves 4

When walking the streets of the cities of Greece, you'd be hard-pressed not to find a shop selling the nation's speciality, souvlaki: tender meat skewers marinated in a herb, lemon and oil dressing. Soak 8 bamboo skewers in water for at least 30 minutes before using to prevent scorching and splintering.

¼ cup (60ml) olive oil
2 teaspoons finely grated lemon rind
¼ cup (60ml) lemon juice
¼ cup finely chopped fresh oregano
800g fillets, cut into 3cm pieces
2 medium yellow capsicums (400g),
    chopped coarsely
1 medium red onion (150g),
    chopped coarsely
2 large tomatoes (440g), chopped coarsely
¼ cup (35g) roasted slivered almonds
1 cup firmly packed fresh mint leaves

1 Combine oil, rind, juice and oregano in screw-top jar; shake well.
2 Thread lamb, capsicum and onion, alternately, on skewers. Place on baking tray; drizzle with half the dressing. Cook souvlaki on heated oiled grill plate (or grill or barbecue) until cooked as desired.
3 Meanwhile, combine tomato, nuts and mint with the remaining dressing in small bowl.
4 Serve souvlaki with tomato, almond and mint salad, and pitta bread, if desired.

per serving 26.1g total fat (5.5g saturated fat); 1914kJ (458 cal); 7.8g carbohydrate; 46.2g protein; 4.3g fibre

warm pasta provençale salad

prep time 15 minutes   cook time 15 minutes   serves 6

All the flavours of the sunny south of France skyrocket in this salad. Rigatoni, a tube-shaped pasta with ridges on the outside, is ideal used in this salad: its wide hollow centre captures the dish's other ingredients and the dressing clings to the pasta's indentations. You can use black olive tapenade in this recipe, if you prefer.

375g rigatoni
600g fillets
¾ cup (115g) seeded black olives, halved
1 cup (150g) drained semi-dried tomatoes
   in oil, chopped coarsely
400g can artichoke hearts, drained, halved
1 small red onion (100g), sliced thinly
60g baby rocket leaves
½ cup (120g) green olive tapenade
2 tablespoons olive oil
2 tablespoons lemon juice

1 Cook pasta in large saucepan of boiling water until tender.
2 Meanwhile, cook lamb, uncovered, in heated oiled large frying pan until cooked as desired. Cover; stand 5 minutes then slice thickly.
3 Combine drained pasta with lamb and remaining ingredients in large bowl. Serve warm.

per serving 16.9g total fat (3.4g saturated fat); 2203kJ (527 cal); 57.4g carbohydrate; 32g protein; 7.5g fibre

lamb char siu stir-fry

prep time 15 minutes   cook time 20 minutes   serves 4

2 tablespoons rice vinegar
2 tablespoons peanut oil
2 tablespoons char siu sauce
1 tablespoon kecap manis
2 cloves garlic, crushed
600g fillets, sliced thickly
1 tablespoon peanut oil, extra
200g broccolini, trimmed
200g snow peas, trimmed
200g sugar snap peas, trimmed
1 fresh long red chilli, sliced thinly

1 Combine vinegar, oil, sauce, kecap manis, garlic and lamb in medium bowl. Drain lamb; reserve sauce mixture.
2 Cook lamb, in batches, in heated oiled wok until browned.
3 Heat extra oil in cleaned wok; stir-fry broccolini and peas, in batches. Return vegetables and lamb to wok with reserved sauce mixture; stir-fry until hot. Serve sprinkled with chilli.
per serving 19.6g total fat (4.9g saturated fat); 1517kJ (363 cal); 7.9g carbohydrate; 36.8g protein; 4.6g fibre

grilled lamb with paprikash sauce

prep time 5 minutes   cook time 10 minutes   serves 4

800g backstraps
1 tablespoon olive oil
1 small brown onion (80g), chopped finely
1 clove garlic, crushed
1 teaspoon smoked paprika
2 teaspoons sweet paprika
pinch cayenne pepper
410g can crushed tomatoes
½ cup (125ml) water

1 Cook lamb on heated oiled grill plate (or grill or barbecue). Cover; stand 5 minutes then slice thickly.
2 Meanwhile, heat oil in medium saucepan; cook onion, stirring, until onion softens. Add garlic and spices; cook, stirring, about 1 minute or until fragrant.
3 Add undrained tomatoes and the water; bring to a boil. Reduce heat; simmer, uncovered, about 5 minutes or until paprikash sauce thickens slightly.
4 Serve lamb with sauce, and baked potatoes, if desired.
per serving 12g total fat (3.8g saturated fat); 1241kJ (297 cal); 4.4g carbohydrate; 42.1g protein; 1.6g fibre

prosciutto-wrapped lamb with minted pea sauce

prep time 15 minutes cook time 20 minutes serves 4

4 slices prosciutto (60g)

4 x 200g backstraps

2 teaspoons olive oil

20g butter

1 shallot (25g), chopped finely

1 clove garlic, crushed

1 rindless bacon rasher (65g), sliced thinly

2 teaspoons plain flour

¼ cup (60ml) dry white wine

⅓ cup (80ml) chicken stock

¼ cup (30g) frozen peas

2 tablespoons cream

1 tablespoon finely chopped fresh mint

1 Wrap one slice of prosciutto around each backstrap. Heat oil in large frying pan; cook lamb until cooked as desired. Cover; stand 5 minutes then slice thickly.

2 Meanwhile, melt butter in same pan; cook onion, garlic and bacon until onion softens. Add flour; cook, stirring, 1 minute.

3 Stir in wine; bring to a boil. Reduce heat; simmer, stirring, until mixture boils and thickens. Stir in stock and peas; bring to a boil. Reduce heat; simmer, uncovered, until mixture reduces by half. Stir in cream.

4 Blend or process mixture until smooth; stir in mint. Serve lamb with minted pea sauce, and steamed broccolini, if desired.

per serving 20.3g total fat (9.9g saturated fat); 1651kJ (395 cal); 2.6g carbohydrate; 48g protein; 0.7g fibre

thyme-scented lamb with almond skordalia

prep time 10 minutes   cook time 40 minutes   serves 4

Skordalia is a classic Greek accompaniment served with grilled meats and seafood. Traditionally, it can be made either with ground nuts or pureed potato, but garlic, lemon juice and olive oil are deliciously present in all variations.

700g desiree potatoes, cut into 2cm pieces
2 medium red capsicums (400g),
   chopped coarsely
1 tablespoon olive oil
2 teaspoons fresh thyme leaves
4 x 200g backstraps
almond skordalia
⅔ cup (80g) almond meal
½ cup (35g) stale breadcrumbs
2 cloves garlic, crushed
2 tablespoons lemon juice
⅔ cup (160ml) olive oil

1   Preheat oven to 220°C/200°C fan-forced.
2   Combine potato, capsicum, oil and thyme in large shallow baking dish. Roast, covered, 20 minutes. Uncover; roast 15 minutes.
3   Meanwhile, cook lamb in heated oiled large frying pan. Cover; stand 5 minutes then slice thickly.
4   Make almond skordalia.
5   Serve sliced lamb with potato, capsicum and skordalia.

almond skordalia   Blend or process almond meal, breadcrumbs, garlic and juice until combined. With motor operating, gradually add oil in a thin, steady stream until skordalia is smooth and creamy.

per serving 59.9g total fat (9.8g saturated fat); 3716kJ (889 cal); 33.6g carbohydrate; 52g protein; 6.9g fibre

tandoori lamb pizza

prep time **10 minutes** cook time **30 minutes** serves **4**

We used large, 25cm diameter, packaged pizza bases for this recipe.

¼ cup (70g) yogurt
¼ cup (75g) tandoori paste
600g backstraps
30g butter
2 medium red onions (300g), sliced thickly
1 clove garlic, crushed
2 x 335g pizza bases
½ cup (160g) mango chutney
⅓ cup (50g) coarsely chopped raisins
¼ cup (70g) yogurt, extra
⅓ cup loosely packed fresh
  coriander leaves

1 Preheat oven to 220°C/200°C fan-forced.
2 Combine yogurt, paste and lamb in medium bowl.
3 Heat butter in medium saucepan; cook onion and garlic, stirring, about 15 minutes or until onion is caramelised.
4 Place pizza bases on oven trays; spread each with chutney then top with onion and raisins. Cook about 15 minutes or until bases are crisp.
5 Meanwhile, cook lamb on heated oiled grill plate (or grill or barbecue) until cooked as desired. Cover; stand 5 minutes then slice thinly.
6 Top pizzas with lamb, extra yogurt and coriander.
per serving 25.2g total fat (8.7g saturated fat); 3954kJ (946 cal); 112.7g carbohydrate; 50.3g protein; 10.9g fibre

honey and five-spice lamb with buk choy

prep time 15 minutes cook time 10 minutes serves 4

¼ teaspoon five-spice powder

¼ cup (60ml) oyster sauce

2 tablespoons honey

2 tablespoons rice vinegar

2 cloves garlic, crushed

600g fillets, sliced thinly

400g fresh thin rice noodles

1 tablespoon sesame oil

2 fresh long red chillies, sliced thinly

2cm piece fresh ginger (10g), cut
   into matchsticks

1 medium red onion (150g), sliced thickly

500g baby buk choy, leaves separated

¼ cup firmly packed fresh coriander leaves

1 tablespoon crushed peanuts

1 Combine five-spice, sauce, honey, vinegar and garlic in small bowl.

2 Combine lamb with 1 tablespoon of the five-spice mixture in medium bowl.

3 Place noodles in large heatproof bowl, cover with boiling water; separate noodles with fork, drain.

4 Heat oil in wok; stir-fry lamb, in batches, until browned. Return to wok; add remaining five-spice mixture, chilli, ginger and onion; stir-fry until onion softens. Add noodles and buk choy; stir-fry until hot.

5 Serve stir-fry sprinkled with coriander and nuts.

per serving 12.2g total fat (3.3g saturated fat); 1781kJ (426 cal); 40.7g carbohydrate; 36.1g protein; 3.3g fibre

lamb, fetta and spinach fillo parcels

prep time **25 minutes** cook time **25 minutes** serves 4

You need 2 bunches of spinach weighing about 400g each to get the amount of trimmed spinach required for this recipe.

300g trimmed spinach
¾ cup (150g) fetta cheese, crumbled
1 tablespoon fresh oregano leaves
½ teaspoon cracked black pepper
1 teaspoon finely grated lemon rind
8 x 100g fillets
8 sheets fillo pastry
cooking-oil spray

1 Preheat oven to 240°C/220°C fan-forced. Oil oven tray; line with baking paper.

2 Boil, steam or microwave spinach until tender; drain. Rinse under cold water; drain well. Chop spinach coarsely; combine in medium bowl with cheese, oregano, pepper and rind.

3 Cook lamb, in batches, in heated oiled large frying pan until browned.

4 Stack four fillo sheets, spraying individual sheets lightly with oil. Cut fillo stack in half widthways; cover with a slightly damp tea towel to prevent drying out. Repeat process with remaining four fillo sheets; you will have four fillo stacks.

5 Uncover one fillo stack; place on board. Centre two fillets on stack, top fillets with a quarter of the spinach mixture. Roll stack to enclose filling, folding in sides after first complete turn of roll. Spray parcel with cooking-oil spray; place on tray. Repeat process with remaining three fillo stacks, lamb and spinach.

6 Bake parcels, in oven, about 15 minutes or until fillo is browned lightly. Serve with greek-style yogurt and lemon wedges, if desired.

per serving 19.5g total fat (9.3g saturated fat); 1990kJ (476 cal); 20.5g carbohydrate; 53.1g protein; 3g fibre

Each of these recipes serves 4, and can be on the table in 30 minutes or less.

za'atar-crumbed backstrap

Blend or process 2 tablespoons za'atar and ⅓ cup coarsely chopped roasted unsalted cashews until mixture resembles coarse breadcrumbs. Combine 800g backstraps with 2 tablespoons olive oil in large bowl; add za'atar mixture, turn lamb to coat all over. Heat 1 tablespoon olive oil in large frying pan; cook lamb, in batches, until cooked as desired. Cover; stand 5 minutes then slice thickly. Goes well with lemon and parsley couscous.

lebanese grilled lamb wraps

Cook 1 thickly sliced red capsicum and 3 thickly lengthways-sliced zucchini on heated oiled grill plate until tender. Rub four 100g fillets with 2 tablespoons sumac; grill until cooked as desired. Cover; stand 5 minutes then slice thickly. Chop ¼ cup each fresh mint and fresh flat-leaf parsley. Spread ⅓ cup baba ghanoush on each of 4 large warmed pitta breads; top with lamb, zucchini, capsicum and herb mixture. Top each with a tablespoon of yogurt; roll tightly. Serve cut in half on the diagonal.

lamb with pecan tomato salsa

Combine 2 tablespoons each olive oil and balsamic vinegar, 1 crushed garlic clove, 2 teaspoons grated lemon rind, 1 cup chopped roasted pecans, 2 chopped seeded small tomatoes, 1 chopped medium red onion and ½ cup chopped fresh flat-leaf parsley in medium bowl. Meanwhile, cook 800g backstraps on heated oiled grill plate (or grill or barbecue) until cooked as desired. Cover; stand 5 minutes then slice thickly. Serve topped with salsa. Goes well with steamed basmati and wild rice blend.

lamb & rocket bruschetta

Heat oiled medium frying pan; cook 600g backstraps, until cooked as desired. Cover; stand 5 minutes then slice thinly. Meanwhile, cut ½ loaf ciabatta into 8 slices; toast slices both sides. Rub 1 side of slices with a little crushed garlic then spread with ⅓ cup sun-dried tomato pesto. Top with ¼ cup mayonnaise combined with 2 teaspoons dijon mustard. Divide sliced lamb among bruschetta; sprinkle with 25g baby rocket leaves.

backstrap with mint pesto

Blend or process 2 cups firmly packed fresh mint leaves, 2 quartered cloves garlic, ⅓ cup roasted unsalted pistachios, ⅓ cup olive oil and 2 tablespoons coarsely grated parmesan cheese until mixture forms a paste. Cook 800g backstraps on heated oiled grill plate (or grill or barbecue) until cooked as desired. Cover; stand 5 minutes then slice thickly. Serve with mint pesto. Goes well with sliced roast potato.

sesame, chilli & parsley lamb

Combine ½ cup toasted sesame seeds, ½ teaspoon dried chilli flakes and 2 tablespoons finely chopped fresh flat-leaf parsley in small bowl. Combine 800g backstraps with 2 tablespoons olive oil in large bowl; add sesame parsley mixture, turn lamb to coat all over. Cook lamb on heated oiled grill plate (or grill or barbecue) until browned all over and cooked as desired. Cover; stand 5 minutes then slice thickly. Goes well with tomato, basil and bocconcini salad.

skewers & capsicum sauce

Roast, then peel 3 quartered medium red capsicum. Process capsicum, 2 quartered cloves garlic, ¼ cup fresh basil leaves and 2 teaspoons balsamic vinegar until smooth. Cut 800g fillets into 3cm cubes; thread onto 8 pre-soaked bamboo skewers. Cook skewers on heated oiled grill plate (or grill or barbecue). Serve skewers with red capsicum dipping sauce and watercress. Goes well with guacamole and tortillas.

sumac-oregano fillets

Combine 1 tablespoon each sumac and dried oregano with 1 cup stale breadcrumbs in shallow medium bowl. Beat 1 egg in another shallow medium bowl. Place ¼ cup plain flour in a third shallow medium bowl. Dip six 100g fillets in flour then coat in egg and finally in spice mixture. Heat ¼ cup olive oil in large frying pan; cook lamb until cooked as desired. Cover; stand 5 minutes then slice thickly. Goes well with a lebanese salad such as tabbouleh or fattoush.

Pork fillets

This low-fat fillet scores big points in the health department. Gone are the days of boring, dry pork – we've entered a new era with succulent, tender cuts that taste great stir-fried, with pasta and in salads.

cashew, lemon and thyme crumbed schnitzel

prep time **20 minutes** cook time **15 minutes** serves **4**

4 x 150g medallions
1 cup (150g) roasted unsalted cashews
½ cup (35g) stale breadcrumbs
2 teaspoons finely grated lemon rind
2 teaspoons finely chopped fresh thyme
1 egg
vegetable oil, for shallow-frying
1 medium lemon (140g), quartered

1 Using meat mallet, gently pound pork, one piece at a time, between sheets of plastic wrap, until about 5mm in thickness.
2 Blend or process nuts until coarsely chopped; combine in shallow medium bowl with breadcrumbs, rind and thyme. Whisk egg lightly in another shallow medium bowl. Dip pork in egg then coat in cashew mixture.
3 Heat oil in large frying pan; cook pork, in batches. Drain on absorbent paper. Serve pork with lemon.
per serving 38.5g total fat (6.8g saturated); 2391kJ (572 cal); 13g carbohydrate; 42.5g protein; 3.3g fibre

stir-fried pork with buk choy and rice noodles

prep time 10 minutes cook time 10 minutes serves 4

¼ cup (60ml) oyster sauce

2 tablespoons light soy sauce

2 tablespoons sweet sherry

1 tablespoon brown sugar

1 clove garlic, crushed

1 star anise, crushed

pinch five-spice powder

400g fresh rice noodles

2 teaspoons sesame oil

600g fillets, sliced thinly

700g baby buk choy, chopped coarsely

1 Combine sauces, sherry, sugar, garlic, star anise and five-spice in small jug.

2 Place noodles in large heatproof bowl, cover with boiling water; separate with fork, drain.

3 Heat oil in wok; stir-fry pork, in batches, until cooked as desired. Return pork to wok with sauce mixture, noodles and buk choy; stir-fry until buk choy is wilted.

per serving 6.7g total fat (1.6g saturated fat); 1492kJ (357 cal); 31.6g carbohydrate; 37.9g protein; 2.9g fibre

coconut and lemon grass pork and mushroom soup

prep time 10 minutes cook time 20 minutes serves 4

1 litre (4 cups) chicken stock

2 x 140ml cans coconut milk

10cm stick fresh lemon grass (20g),
  chopped finely

5cm piece fresh ginger (25g),
  chopped finely

1 clove garlic, crushed

2 teaspoons fish sauce

600g fillets, sliced thinly

300g oyster mushrooms, halved

2 fresh long red chillies, sliced thinly

1 tablespoon lime juice

4 green onions, sliced thinly

1 Combine stock, coconut milk, lemon grass, ginger, garlic and sauce in large saucepan; bring to a boil. Reduce heat; simmer, covered, 10 minutes.

2 Add pork, mushroom, chilli and juice; return to a boil. Reduce heat; simmer, covered, until pork is cooked. Serve soup sprinkled with onion.

per serving 19.2g total fat (14.4g saturated fat); 1517kJ (363 cal); 5.8g carbohydrate; 39.9g protein; 5g fibre

pork red curry with green apple

prep time 15 minutes cook time 20 minutes serves 4

We used a prepared red curry paste for this recipe as its particular blend of flavours complements the pork especially well.

¼ cup (60ml) peanut oil
600g fillets
¼ cup (75g) red curry paste
1 medium brown onion (150g),
  chopped coarsely
4cm piece fresh ginger (20g), grated
400ml can coconut milk
⅔ cup (160ml) chicken stock
3 medium green apples (450g)
½ cup (70g) roasted unsalted peanuts
½ cup coarsely chopped thai basil

1 Heat half the oil in large saucepan; cook pork, uncovered, until browned. Remove from heat; set aside.

2 Heat remaining oil in same cleaned pan; cook paste, onion and ginger, stirring, until onion softens. Add coconut milk and stock; bring to a boil. Reduce heat; simmer, uncovered, 5 minutes.

3 Meanwhile, peel, core and thinly slice apples. Return pork to pan with apple; simmer, covered, about 10 minutes or until apple softens. Remove from heat; remove pork, slice thickly.

4 Divide pork among bowls; top with curry mixture then sprinkle with nuts and basil.

per serving 52.3g total fat (23.5g saturated fat); 3085kJ (719 cal); 18.5g carbohydrate; 41.4g protein; 7.3g fibre

grilled medallions with capsicum cream sauce

prep time 15 minutes cook time 15 minutes serves 4

1 medium red capsicum (200g)
1 medium tomato (150g), halved, seeded
2 teaspoons olive oil
1 clove garlic, crushed
1 small brown onion (80g), chopped finely
½ trimmed celery stalk (50g), chopped finely
2 tablespoons water
1 teaspoon finely chopped fresh rosemary
4 x 150g medallions
½ cup (125ml) cream

1 Quarter capsicum; discard seeds and membranes. Roast capsicum and tomato under grill or in very hot oven, skin-side up, until capsicum skin blisters and blackens. Cover capsicum and tomato pieces with plastic or paper for 5 minutes; peel away skins then slice capsicum thickly.

2 Heat oil in large frying pan; cook garlic, onion and celery until softened. Add capsicum, tomato and the water; cook, uncovered, 5 minutes. Remove from heat; stir in rosemary.

3 Meanwhile, cook pork on heated oiled grill plate (or grill or barbecue) until cooked as desired. Cover to keep warm.

4 Blend or process capsicum mixture until smooth. Return to same pan, add cream; bring to a boil. Reduce heat; simmer, uncovered, 5 minutes. Serve pork with sauce.

per serving 19.4g total fat (10.5g saturated fat); 1404kJ (336 cal); 4.7g carbohydrate; 35g protein; 1.8g fibre

roasted pork fillet with pear and apricot relish

prep time 10 minutes cook time 20 minutes serves 4

410g can sliced pears in natural juice
410g can apricot halves in natural juice
600g fillets
1 tablespoon olive oil
½ cup (125ml) water
2 tablespoons white vinegar
1 fresh long red chilli, chopped finely
¼ cup (40g) sultanas
2 tablespoons white sugar

1 Preheat oven to 240°C/220°C fan-forced.

2 Drain pears over small bowl. Reserve juice; chop pears coarsely. Drain apricots, discarding juice. Chop apricots coarsely.

3 Place pork in oiled baking dish; drizzle with oil. Roast, uncovered, about 20 minutes or until cooked as desired. Cover; stand 5 minutes then slice thickly.

4 Meanwhile, combine pear, apricot, reserved juice and remaining ingredients in medium saucepan; bring to a boil. Reduce heat; simmer, uncovered, about 20 minutes or until relish thickens slightly. Serve pork with relish and steamed snow peas, if desired.

per serving 8g total fat (1.8g saturated fat); 1400kJ (335 cal); 29.2g carbohydrate; 34.2g protein; 3.3g fibre

sliced pan-fried fillet with carrot and potato mash

prep time 10 minutes   cook time 25 minutes   serves 4

700g potatoes, chopped coarsely
2 medium carrots (240g), chopped coarsely
50g butter
600g fillets
4 shallots (100g), halved
2 medium apples (300g)
²⁄₃ cup (160ml) ginger beer
1 tablespoon lime marmalade

1 Boil, steam or microwave potato and carrot, separately, until tender; drain. Mash potato and carrot in large bowl with half the butter until smooth; cover to keep warm.

2 Heat remaining butter in large frying pan. Cook pork and shallot, uncovered, stirring occasionally, until pork is cooked as desired. Cover to keep warm.

3 Meanwhile, peel, core and thinly slice apples. Combine in medium saucepan with ginger beer and marmalade; bring to a boil. Reduce heat; simmer, uncovered, about 10 minutes or until apple softens.

4 Serve sliced pork with shallot, apple and mash.

per serving 14g total fat (8g saturated fat); 1914kJ (458cal); 45.3g carbohydrate; 38.1g protein; 6.4g fibre

warm pork and mandarin salad with honey dressing

prep time 10 minutes cook time 10 minutes serves 4

600g fillets
2 medium mandarins (400g), peeled
2 tablespoons olive oil
1 tablespoon honey
1 fresh long red chilli, chopped finely
2 medium radicchio (400g), trimmed
1 cup (50g) snow pea sprouts
¾ cup (115g) roasted unsalted cashews

1 Cook pork, uncovered, in heated oiled large frying pan until cooked as desired. Cover; stand 5 minutes then slice thickly.

2 Meanwhile, segment mandarins into large bowl. Add oil, honey and chilli; stir gently to combine. Add pork, radicchio, sprouts and nuts; toss salad, serve warm.

per serving 27.2g total fat (5g saturated fat); 2098kJ (502 cal); 20.7g carbohydrate; 41g protein; 5.9g fibre

pork fillets with craisin crumb topping and red wine sauce

prep time 20 minutes   cook time 20 minutes   serves 4

1 tablespoon olive oil
1 medium brown onion (150g),
   chopped finely
1 clove garlic, crushed
2 tablespoons craisins
60g baby spinach leaves
½ cup (35g) stale breadcrumbs
¼ cup (40g) roasted pine nuts
600g fillets
½ cup (125ml) dry red wine
¾ cup (180ml) chicken stock
2 tablespoons redcurrant jelly

1 Heat oil in large frying pan; cook onion and garlic, stirring, until onion softens. Add craisins and spinach; cook, stirring, until spinach wilts. Combine craisin mixture with breadcrumbs and nuts in medium bowl. Cover to keep warm.

2 Cook pork, uncovered, in same pan until cooked as desired. Cover; stand 5 minutes then slice thickly.

3 Meanwhile, bring wine to a boil in small saucepan. Reduce heat; simmer, uncovered, until reduced by half. Add stock and jelly; cook, uncovered, about 10 minutes, stirring occasionally, or until sauce thickens.

4 Serve pork with craisin crumb topping and drizzled with sauce.

per serving 15.6g total fat (2.4g saturated fat); 1689kJ (404 cal); 22.2g carbohydrate; 37.1g protein; 2.6g fibre

pork, rocket and sopressa pasta

prep time 15 minutes cook time 20 minutes serves 4

Sopressa, a salami from the north of Italy, can be found in both mild and chilli-flavoured varieties. If you can't find it easily, you can use any hot salami, but the taste won't be exactly the same.

100g baby rocket leaves

¼ cup (60ml) olive oil

2 tablespoons lemon juice

375g fettuccine

600g fillets

1 medium brown onion (150g),
  chopped finely

1 clove garlic, crushed

100g hot sopressa, sliced thinly

1 Blend or process rocket, oil and juice until rocket is finely chopped.

2 Cook pasta in large saucepan of boiling water, uncovered, until tender.

3 Meanwhile, cook pork, uncovered, in heated oiled large frying pan, until cooked as desired. Remove from pan; cover to keep warm.

4 Cook onion, garlic and salami in same pan, stirring, until onion softens.

5 Combine drained pasta in large bowl with thinly sliced pork, and rocket and salami mixtures.

per serving 27.8g total fat (6.4g saturated fat); 3047kJ (729 cal); 67.2g carbohydrate; 50.1g protein; 4.1g fibre

Each of these recipes serves 4, and can be on the table in 30 minutes or less.

char siu pork salad

Grate 1 teaspoon rind from 1 of 2 large oranges; segment both oranges over large bowl. Reserve ⅓ cup juice; discard remainder. Combine 2 tablespoons reserved juice with rind, ¼ cup char siu sauce,1 finely chopped fresh red thai chilli and 600g fillets in medium bowl. Cook pork, uncovered, in heated oiled wok. Cover; stand 5 minutes then slice thickly. Place pork in bowl with orange segments; mix in remaining juice, 2 tablespoons olive oil and 200g mizuna. Serve topped with ¼ cup chopped roasted unsalted peanuts.

tamarind & date pork braise

Heat 1 tablespoon olive oil in large frying pan; cook 600g thinly sliced fillets, in batches, until browned. Cook 1 finely chopped fresh long red chilli and 1 finely chopped shallot in same pan until softened. Return pork to pan with ½ cup tamarind and date chutney and ⅓ cup water; bring to a boil. Reduce heat; simmer, covered, about 5 minutes or until pork is cooked as desired. Goes well with steamed jasmine rice and stir-fried choy sum in oyster sauce.

pan-fried fillets & pear chips

Cook 600g fillets, uncovered, in heated large oiled frying pan until cooked as desired. Cover; stand 5 minutes then slice thickly. Add 1 cup pear juice, 1 tablespoon balsamic vinegar and 1 finely chopped fresh long red chilli to same pan; bring to a boil. Reduce heat; simmer about 5 minutes or until liquid reduces by half. Remove sauce from pan; keep warm. Slice 1 medium pear with V-slicer or mandoline. Heat ¼ cup vegetable oil in same cleaned pan; shallow-fry pear slices, in batches, until crisp. Drain; serve chips with pork and sauce.

honey & ginger pork

Combine 2 tablespoons each japanese soy sauce, mirin and honey in small jug with ¼ cup water, 2 teaspoons sesame oil, 2 crushed garlic cloves and 4cm piece grated fresh ginger. Meanwhile, heat 1 tablespoon sesame oil in wok; stir-fry 600g thinly sliced fillets, in batches, until browned. Stir-fry 1 thinly sliced small red onion and 150g trimmed sugar snap peas until tender. Return pork to wok with sauce mixture; stir-fry until pork is cooked as desired. Goes well with hot hokkien noodles.

grilled pork & salsa verde

Combine 1 cup chopped fresh flat-leaf parsley, ½ cup chopped fresh mint, 2 tablespoons each lemon juice and rinsed baby capers, 1 crushed garlic clove and ¼ cup olive oil in small bowl. Combine 600g fillets in large bowl with 2 crushed garlic cloves, 2 tablespoons olive oil and 2 teaspoons each finely grated lemon rind and lemon juice. Cook pork on heated oiled grill plate. Cover; stand 5 minutes then slice thinly. Serve with salsa verde. Goes well with steamed rice and lemon wedges.

harissa & lime-rubbed pork

Combine ½ cup harissa paste, 2 teaspoons finely grated lime rind, 1 tablespoon lime juice, 1 crushed garlic clove and 600g fillets in large bowl. Heat 1 tablespoon olive oil in large frying pan; cook pork, uncovered, until browned all over. Cover pork; cook about 10 minutes or until cooked as desired. Remove pan from heat; stand pork, covered, 5 minutes then slice thickly. Goes well with couscous tossed with lemon juice, parsley and pine nuts.

plum & soy wok-fried pork

Heat 1 tablespoon peanut oil in wok; stir-fry 600g thinly sliced fillets, in batches, until browned. Heat another tablespoon peanut oil in same wok; stir-fry 1 thickly sliced large brown onion and 1 crushed garlic clove 1 minute. Add 340g trimmed asparagus and 2 sliced medium red capsicums; stir-fry until softened. Return pork to wok with combined ½ cup plum sauce and 2 tablespoons light soy sauce; stir-fry until pork is cooked as desired. Goes well with steamed jasmine rice.

pork with grapefruit olive salsa

Segment one medium yellow grapefruit and one medium red grapefruit into medium bowl. Reserve 2 tablespoons juice; discard remainder. Chop grapefruit segments coarsely then stir in 100g finely chopped green olives, 1 finely chopped fresh long red chilli, 1 finely chopped small red onion, 1 teaspoon olive oil and 1 teaspoon sugar. Heat 1 tablespoon olive oil in large frying pan; cook 600g thickly sliced fillets, uncovered, until cooked as desired. Serve pork with salsa. Goes well with roasted kipfler potatoes.

Glossary

ALMOND

flaked paper-thin slices.

meal also known as ground almonds; nuts are powdered to a coarse flour texture for use in baking or as a thickening agent.

BAMBOO SHOOTS tender, pale yellow, edible first-growth of the bamboo plant. Available fresh in Asian greengrocers in season, but usually purchased canned; must be drained and rinsed before use.

BARBECUE SAUCE spicy, tomato-based sauce used to baste or as an accompaniment.

BLACK BEAN SAUCE an Asian cooking sauce made from salted and fermented soybeans, spices and wheat flour.

BUK CHOY also known as bok choy, pak choi, chinese white cabbage or chinese chard; has a fresh, mild mustard taste. *Baby buk choy*, also known as pak kat farang or shanghai bok choy, is smaller and more tender than buk choy.

CAPERS the grey-green buds of a warm climate (usually Mediterranean) shrub; sold either dried and salted or pickled in a vinegar brine. Tiny young ones, called *baby capers*, are also available both in brine or dried in salt.

CHAR SIU SAUCE also known as chinese barbecue sauce; a paste-like ingredient that has a sharp, sweet and spicy flavour. Made with fermented soybeans, honey and spices.

CHEESE

bocconcini walnut sized, baby mozzarella; a delicate, semi-soft, white cheese traditionally made from buffalo milk. It spoils rapidly so will only keep, refrigerated in brine, for 2 days.

goat made from goat milk; has an earthy, strong taste. Available in soft, crumbly and firm textures; sometimes rolled in ash or herbs.

parmesan also known as parmigiano; is a hard, grainy cow-milk cheese.

pecorino the generic Italian name for cheeses made from sheep milk. A hard, white to pale-yellow cheese; parmesan can be substituted, if preferred.

ricotta a soft, white, sweet, moist cow-milk cheese with a slightly grainy texture.

CHILLI

flakes also sold as crushed chilli; dehydrated deep-red fine slices and whole seeds.

long green any unripened chilli; also some particular varieties that are ripe when green, such as jalapeño, habanero or serrano.

long red available both fresh and dried; a generic term used for any moderately hot, long, thin chilli (about 6cm to 8cm long).

red thai also known as "scuds"; tiny, very hot and bright red in colour.

CIABATTA a popular Italian crisp-crusted, open-textured white sourdough bread.

COCONUT

cream obtained commercially from the first pressing of the coconut flesh alone, without the addition of water. Available in cans and cartons at most supermarkets.

milk not the liquid found inside the fruit, which is called coconut water, but the diluted liquid from the second pressing of the white flesh of a mature coconut. Available in cans and cartons at most supermarkets.

CRAISINS dried sweetened cranberries.

CURRY PASTE

green hottest of the traditional thai pastes; a hot blend of green chillies, garlic, shallot, lemon grass, salt, galangal, shrimp paste, kaffir lime peel, coriander seed, pepper, cumin and turmeric.

red a medium-hot blend of chilli, garlic, salt, onion, lemon grass, spice and galangal.

tikka a medium-mild paste consisting of chilli, coriander, cumin, lentil flour, garlic, ginger, oil, turmeric, fennel, pepper, cloves, cinnamon and cardamom.

DUKKAH an Egyptian blend of nuts, spices and seeds; is used as a dip or sprinkled over foods as a flavour-enhancer. Available from delicatessens, specialty spice shops and Middle Eastern grocery stores.

FENNEL also known as finocchio or anise; a crunchy green vegetable. Also the name given to the dried seeds of the plant, which have a strong licorice flavour.

FISH, GENERAL

barramundi an Aboriginal word meaning "river fish with large scales".

blue-eye also known as deep sea trevalla or trevally and blue-eye cod; thick, moist white-fleshed fish.

flathead there are many varieties; most common is the dusky flathead, which is also the largest. Substitute with whiting or your favourite white fish.

john dory a pearly-white firm fleshed fish.

kingfish (yellowtail) also known as southern yellowfish, kingie and tasmanian yellowtail. Substitute with dhufish.

ling a member of the cod family, ling are eel-like fish found around rocky locations.

ocean trout a farmed fish with pink, soft flesh; from the same family as atlantic salmon, one can be substituted for the other.

perch also known as coral, red or sea perch, or coral cod; white flesh with a delicate flavour. Substitute with snapper.

salmon red-pink firm flesh with few bones; moist, delicate flavour.

FISH SAUCE also called naam pla or nuoc naam. Made from pulverised salted fermented fish (most often anchovies); has a pungent smell and strong taste, so use according to your taste.

FOCCACIA an Italian yeast dough bread, similar to pizza; usually baked as a large disc and flavoured with olive oil, coarse salt, herbs and garlic.

GAI LAN also known as gai larn, chinese broccoli and chinese kale; a green vegetable appreciated more for its stems than its leaves.

GINGER BEER a fizzy beverage produced from ginger and cane sugar.

GREEN ONIONS also known as scallion or, incorrectly, shallot; an immature onion picked before the bulb has formed, having a long, bright-green edible stalk.

HARISSA PASTE a North African paste made from dried red chillies, garlic, olive oil and caraway seeds. Available from Middle Eastern food shops and some supermarkets.

HOISIN SAUCE a thick, sweet and spicy chinese barbecue sauce made from salted fermented soybeans, onions and garlic. Available from Asian food shops and most major supermarkets.

HORSERADISH

cream commercially prepared creamy paste consisting of grated horseradish, vinegar, oil and sugar.

prepared preserved grated horseradish root.

KAFFIR LIME also known as magrood, leech lime or jeruk purut; the wrinkled, bumpy-skinned green fruit of a small citrus tree originally grown in South Africa and South-East Asia. As a rule, only the rind and leaves are used.

KECAP MANIS a dark, thick, sweet soy sauce; the sweetness is derived from the addition of either molasses or palm sugar when brewed.

LEMON GRASS a tall, clumping, lemon-smelling and tasting tropical grass; the white lower part of the stem is used, finely chopped, in cooking. Available from supermarkets, greengrocers and Asian food shops.

MANDARINS also known as tangerine.

MAPLE SYRUP made from sugar cane; also known as golden or pancake syrup. It is not a substitute for pure maple syrup.

MAYONNAISE we use whole-egg mayonnaise in this book.

MEAT, GENERAL
beef eye fillet tenderloin fillet; fine textured, expensive and extremely tender.
beef scotch fillet also known as cube roll; cuts include rib-eye and standing rib roast.
chicken breast fillet breast halved, skinned and boned.
chicken thigh fillet thigh with skin and centre bone removed.
lamb backstrap also known as eye of loin; the tender, larger fillet from a row of loin chops or cutlets.
lamb fillet fine textured, expensive and extremely tender.
pork fillet boneless eye-fillet.
pork medallions a small trimmed round of meat, slightly greater in thickness but not as large in area, as schnitzel or scaloppine.
prosciutto a kind of unsmoked Italian ham; salted, air-cured and aged.
sopressa a northern-Italian-style hot salami, traditionally flavoured with spices.

MESCLUN pronounced mess-kluhn; also known as mixed greens or spring salad mix. A commercial blend of assorted young lettuce and other green leaves.

MIRIN a Japanese champagne-coloured cooking wine used expressly for cooking; do not confuse with sake. A seasoned sweet mirin, manjo mirin, is also available.

MIZUNA frizzy green salad leaves with a delicate mustard flavour.

MUSHROOMS
flat large, flat mushrooms with a rich, earthy flavour, ideal for filling and barbecuing. They are sometimes misnamed field mushrooms.
oyster also known as abalone; grey-white mushrooms shaped like a fan. Has a smooth texture and a subtle, oyster-like flavour.
swiss brown also known as roman or cremini. Light to dark brown with full-bodied flavour.

MUSTARD, HONEYCUP a tangy mustard made from honey, mustard powder and seeds, spices, oil and vinegar.

OYSTER SAUCE Asian in origin; a thick, richly-flavoured brown sauce made from oysters and their brine, cooked with salt and soy sauce, and thickened with starches.

PAPRIKA ground dried sweet red capsicum (bell pepper); there are many grades and types, including sweet, hot, mild and smoked.

PEPITAS the pale green kernels of dried pumpkin seeds.

PLUM SAUCE a thick, sweet and sour dipping sauce made from plums, vinegar, sugar, chillies and spices.

PIDE also known as turkish bread. Comes in long (about 45cm) flat loaves as well as individual rounds; made from wheat flour.

POLENTA also known as cornmeal; a flour-like cereal made of dried corn (maize). Also the name of the dish made from it.

PUFF PASTRY, READY ROLLED sheets of frozen puff pastry available from supermarkets.

RADICCHIO Italian in origin; a member of the chicory family. Has dark burgundy leaves and a strong, bitter flavour.

REDCURRANT JELLY a preserve made from redcurrants; used as a glaze or in sauces.

RICE NOODLES
dried also known as rice stick noodles. Made from rice flour and water; available flat and wide or very thin (vermicelli). Must be soaked in boiling water to soften.
fresh also known as ho fun, khao pun, sen yau, pho or kway tiau, depending on the country of manufacture. Can be purchased in strands of various widths or large sheets weighing about 500g, which are cut into the desired noodle size.

ROCKET also known as arugula, rugula and rucola; a peppery green leaf. *Baby rocket leaves* are smaller and less peppery.

SAMBAL OELEK (also spelled ulek or olek); Indonesian in origin, this is a salty paste made from ground chillies and vinegar.

SICHUAN PEPPERCORNS also known as szechuan or chinese pepper. Its small, red-brown aromatic sichuan berries have a distinctive peppery-lemon flavour and aroma.

SHALLOTS also called french shallots, golden shallots or eschalots.

SOY SAUCE made from fermented soybeans. Several variations are available in most supermarkets and Asian food stores.

STAR ANISE a dried star-shaped pod with an astringent aniseed flavour.

SUGAR we used coarse, granulated table sugar, also known as crystal sugar, unless otherwise specified.

SULTANAS also known as golden raisins; dried seedless white grapes.

SUMAC a purple-red, astringent spice ground from berries growing on shrubs around the Mediterranean; adds a tart, lemony flavour to food.

TACO SEASONING MIX found in most supermarkets; is meant to duplicate the taste of a Mexican sauce made from oregano, cumin, chillies and other spices.

TAPENADE a thick, black paste containing black olives, olive oil, capers, anchovies and Mediterranean herbs.

THAI BASIL also known as horapa; has small leaves, purplish stems and a slight licorice or aniseed taste.

TORTILLAS thin, unleavened, round bread originating in Mexico; can be made from either wheat or corn.

VIETNAMESE MINT not a mint at all, but a pungent, peppery narrow-leafed member of the buckwheat family. Available from Asian food stores.

VINEGAR
apple cider made from fermented apples.
balsamic originally from Modena, Italy, there are now many balsamic vinegars on the market ranging in pungency and quality depending on how, and for how long, they have been aged.
red wine made from red wine.
rice wine also known as seasoned rice vinegar; made from fermented rice, sugar and salt. Sherry can be substituted.
white made from distilled grain alcohol.

WITLOF also known as belgian endive. Grown in darkness to prevent it becoming green; looks somewhat like a tightly furled, cream to very light-green cigar.

ZA'ATAR a blend of roasted sesame seeds, sumac and crushed dried herbs. Available in delicatessens and specialty food stores.

ZUCCHINI also known as courgette.

Conversion chart

MEASURES

One Australian metric measuring cup holds approximately 250ml; one Australian metric tablespoon holds 20ml; one Australian metric teaspoon holds 5ml.

The difference between one country's measuring cups and another's is within a two- or three-teaspoon variance, and will not affect your cooking results. North America, New Zealand and the United Kingdom use a 15ml tablespoon.

All cup and spoon measurements are level. The most accurate way of measuring dry ingredients is to weigh them. When measuring liquids, use a clear glass or plastic jug with the metric markings.

We use large eggs with an average weight of 60g.

DRY MEASURES

METRIC	IMPERIAL
15g	½oz
30g	1oz
60g	2oz
90g	3oz
125g	4oz (¼lb)
155g	5oz
185g	6oz
220g	7oz
250g	8oz (½lb)
280g	9oz
315g	10oz
345g	11oz
375g	12oz (¾lb)
410g	13oz
440g	14oz
470g	15oz
500g	16oz (1lb)
750g	24oz (1½lb)
1kg	32oz (2lb)

LIQUID MEASURES

METRIC	IMPERIAL
30ml	1 fluid oz
60ml	2 fluid oz
100ml	3 fluid oz
125ml	4 fluid oz
150ml	5 fluid oz (¼ pint/1 gill)
190ml	6 fluid oz
250ml	8 fluid oz
300ml	10 fluid oz (½ pint)
500ml	16 fluid oz
600ml	20 fluid oz (1 pint)
1000ml (1 litre)	1¾ pints

LENGTH MEASURES

METRIC	IMPERIAL
3mm	⅛in
6mm	¼in
1cm	½in
2cm	¾in
2.5cm	1in
5cm	2in
6cm	2½in
8cm	3in
10cm	4in
13cm	5in
15cm	6in
18cm	7in
20cm	8in
23cm	9in
25cm	10in
28cm	11in
30cm	12in (1ft)

OVEN TEMPERATURES

These oven temperatures are only a guide for conventional ovens. For fan-forced ovens, check the manufacturer's manual.

	°C (CELSIUS)	°F (FAHRENHEIT)	GAS MARK
Very slow	120	250	½
Slow	150	275-300	1-2
Moderately slow	160	325	3
Moderate	180	350-375	4-5
Moderately hot	200	400	6
Hot	220	425-450	7-8
Very hot	240	475	9

Index

Book Holder Australia $13.10 (incl. GST). Elsewhere: $A21.95.

Mail or fax Photocopy and complete the coupon below and post to ACP Books Reader Offer, ACP Publishing, GPO Box 4967, Sydney NSW 2001, or fax to (02) 9267 4967.

Phone Have your credit card details ready, then phone 136 116 (within Australia) Mon-Sat, 8.00am-6.00pm.

Australian residents We accept the credit cards listed on the coupon, money orders and cheques.

Overseas residents We accept the credit cards listed on the coupon, drafts in $A drawn on an Australian bank, and also UK, NZ and US cheques in the currency of the country of issue. Credit card charges are at the exchange rate current at the time of payment.

COOKBOOK HOLDERS

Keep your ACP cookbooks clean, tidy and within easy reach with a holder that carries up to 14 books

Photocopy and complete coupon below

Mr/Mrs/Ms _____

Address _____

_____ Postcode _____

Country _____ Phone (business hours) _____

email* (optional) _____

Quantity _____ Total cost $ _____

I enclose my cheque/money order for _____ $ _____

payable to ACP Magazines or please charge_____ $ _____

to my: ☐ Bankcard ☐ Mastercard ☐ Visa ☐ American Express ☐ Diners Club

Expiry date _____

Card number ☐☐☐☐☐☐☐☐☐☐☐☐☐☐☐☐☐☐☐☐

Cardholder's signature _____

* By including your email address, you consent to receipt of any email regarding this magazine, and other emails which inform you of ACP's other publications, products, services and events, and to promote third party goods and services you may be interested in.
Please allow up to 30 days delivery within Australia. Allow up to 6 weeks for overseas delivery.
Offer expires 31/12/07 HL100FF07

If you like this cookbook, you'll love these...

These are just a small selection of titles available in
The Australian Women's Weekly range on sale at selected
newsagents, supermarkets or online at www.acpbooks.com.au

also available in bookstores...

TEST KITCHEN
Food director Pamela Clark
Food editor Karen Hammial
Assistant food editor Sarah Schwikkard
Test Kitchen manager Cathie Lonnie
Senior home economist Elizabeth Macri
Home economists Belinda Farlow, Miranda Farr,
Nicole Jennings, Angela Muscat, Rebecca Squadrito,
Kellie-Marie Thomas, Mary Wills
Nutritional analysis Belinda Farlow

ACP BOOKS
Editorial director Susan Tomnay
Creative director Hieu Chi Nguyen
Designer Hannah Blackmore
Senior editor Wendy Bryant

Director of sales Brian Cearnes
Marketing manager Bridget Cody
Production manager Cedric Taylor

Chief executive officer Ian Law
Group publisher Pat Ingram
General manager Christine Whiston
Editorial director (WW) Deborah Thomas

RIGHTS ENQUIRIES
Laura Bamford Director ACP Books
lbamford@acpuk.com

Produced by ACP Books, Sydney.
Printed by Dai Nippon, c/o Samhwa Printing Co Ltd,
237-10 Kuro-Dong, Kuro-Ku, Seoul, Korea.
Published by ACP Books, a division of
ACP Magazines Ltd, 54 Park St, Sydney;
GPO Box 4088, Sydney, NSW 2001.
phone (02) 9282 8618 fax (02) 9267 9438.
acpbooks@acpmagazines.com.au
www.acpbooks.com.au

To order books, phone 136 116 (within Australia).
Send recipe enquiries to:
recipeenquiries@acpmagazines.com.au

Australia Distributed by Network Services,
phone +61 2 9282 8777 fax +61 2 9264 3278
networkweb@networkservicescompany.com.au
United Kingdom Distributed by Australian
Consolidated Press (UK), phone (01604) 642200
fax (01604) 642300 books@acpuk.com
Canada Distributed by Whitecap Books Ltd,
phone (604) 980 9852 fax (604) 980 8197
customerservice@whitecap.ca
www.whitecap.ca
New Zealand Distributed by Netlink
Distribution Company,
phone (9) 366 9966 ask@ndc.co.nz
South Africa Distributed by PSD Promotions,
phone (27 11) 392 6065/7
fax (27 11) 392 6079/80
orders@psdprom.co.za

The Australian Women's Weekly
Pamela Clark 100 Fast Fillets
Includes index.
ISBN 9 781 86396 5781.
1. Cookery. 2. Meat.
I. Clark, Pamela. II. Title: Australian Women's Weekly.
641.66
© ACP Magazines Ltd 2007
ABN 18 053 273 546

The publishers would like to thank the following
for props used in photography: Maxwell & Williams,
Porter's Paints.